About This Book

Included for your perusal are 42 poems, 87 lyrics, 5 prose pieces you might call "rants," and 49 illustrations. This constitutes my complete literary output and a small part of M.H. Israel's prolific collection.

Each lyric is accompanied by a link to a You Tube performance of the song, and I have included end notes for items whenever I thought comments might be relevant. You will also find brief bios of the author and the illustrator.

Thirty of my songs along with their chord charts and video links are also available as an e-book: "Ukulele Man's Song Book," $1.99   This book too is available as an e-book with all the text and all of M.H. Israel's wonderful illustrations in their full-color beauty, $1.99.

And here are some of my influences:

Dad, Big Billy Goat Gruff, Mom, Horton, "Hippity Hop Bunny," Captain Video, Howdy Doody, Pinky Lee, Captain Kangaroo, Scrooge McDuck, Sister Ann Mary, Alfred E. Newman, Mark Twain, Li'l Abner, Tarzan, Uncle Vern, Turok Son of Stone, Aunt Sis, Laurel & Hardy, Hank, Sally Flowers, Soupy Sales, The Kingston Trio, The Mouseketeers, Pete Seeger, Little Richard, Ed Sullivan, Elvis, Sherlock Holmes, Chuck Berry, the Plymouth, Honorable Ball Peen Man, Woody Guthrie, Edgar Rice Burroughs, the Beatles, Edgar Allen Poe, Dylan, "Brown Eyed Girl," Inherit The Wind, Herman's Hermits, Herman Melville, the DeSoto, the Temple of Psychic Prophecy, The Monkees, the "Jones-Lawrence Memorial Award," Don Quixote, Indian Ike, Twilight Zone, MLK, "The Conqueror Worm," Star Trek, Malcolm X, Robert Frost, Dr. Strangelove, Venice, The Rolling Stones, Fellini, "Ozymandias," Don McLean, Edvard Munch, Animal Farm, Al Crapp, the TR3, Emily Dickinson, Kung Fu, T.S. Elliot, The Crucible, e.e. cummings, Leaves of Grass, Jung, Steven Crane, the Bug, Joe Cocker, Sondra, Brave New World, Carlos Castenada, "Eldorado," Bob & George, New Orleans, Pee-Wee's Playhouse, Kenny Sparky Mona and Ray, John Lennon, Café Du Monde, San Francisco, "The X-Files," Waiting for Godot, Oscar Wilde, the Redwoods, The Simpsons, Manhattan, *the* Eldorado.

I've Never Been to Stuckey's

Well, I'm goin' down the highway goin' my way
Goin' nowhere, goin' fast; oh you gotta be so strong
To keep on keeping on down the highway of life

And the wheels go round and round and round
And they never touch the ground, the ground
Spinnin' nowhere, spinnin' fast
But I know I'm gonna get there, somewhere, if only I can last
On the highway of life

I'm goin' down the highway goin' my way
Goin' nowhere goin' fast; oh, put the pedal to the metal
You know somebody's gonna try and pass
On the highway of life

Look there's a Stuckey's
Maybe we should stop and get a pecan log
Nah, we got time. We've got lots of time
There'll be another Stuckey's down the road

We've got time; you can cut it with a knife
On the highway of life
And the hotrod comes out of nowhere
Goin' nowhere, goin' nowhere, goin' fast
Oh, he hangs there on your bumper
Then he blows out, around, and past
Down the highway of life

And he's goin' nowhere, goin' nowhere, goin' nowhere
Goin' nowhere, just like you and me
But he thinks that when he gets there, he'll be young, tan, and free
On the highway of life

Oh Look! There's another Stuckey's!
Two Stuckey's have emerged in a mellow mood
And I, sad that I could not travel there
Oh, I took the road more traveled by
And I don't think it's made a damned bit of difference
On the highway of life

Oh, I'm goin' down that highway goin' my way
Goin' nowhere, goin' fast; you gotta be so strong
To keep on keeping on down the highway of life

But I know I'm gonna get there, somewhere
With the wind blowin' through my hair
On the highway of life

La-la-la-la-la-la-la-la-la-la-la-la-la-la-

http://www.youtube.com/watch?v=8alFso8JMJg
Search: Ukulele Man - "I've Never Been to Stuckey's"

Bird Man

Traveling in a foreign land
I came across
an old
Bird Man
Who took me in
to his humble home
where with his birds he lived alone

And all that evening his cottage rang
While the birds sat listening and the Old Man
Sang

His song was as strong as an Eagle's cry
As mournful as the gray Dove's sigh
Hypnotic like the great Owl's stare
Haunting as the Loon's fanfare

And the listening birds added not one note
To the song that flew from Human throat

On and on throughout the night
The Old Man spread his voice in flight
Until, near dawn, he did alight
and smiled at me, that Wren-ish sprite
With wizened face but sparkling eyes

Who suddenly
to my surprise
Hopped 'cross his well-worn, littered floor
And opened wide his chamber door

Then the birds
– as men leave church –
Arose as one from off their perch
And through the door into the sky
to fly to soar
Burst through the door to fly, to soar

And then I saw it
(a simple thing) :

Free birds fly; we caged birds sing

http://www.youtube.com/watch?v=t4VP_V207-I
Search: Bird Man - Jeff Hartley music / Tom Harker lyrics

Gemini

Gemini has two faces

                With opposing views
             (sometimes they make the
               effort to commune)

            Mostly

                          One makes demands, and
                          The other makes amends

(neither will let the other rest)

            Indeed !

         One sees what gods see, and
         The other mourns humanity.

                         And whenever

(on those notable occasions)

                        They turn inward upon themselves

          To kiss,

         They bite instead.

Crazy Old World

It's a crazy old world
As crazy as it can be
If you don't think so,
Just take a look at me.

It's a crazy old world
I know it's true
If you don't think so,
Just take a look at you.

I'm just sittin' on the world
And watchin' it go round.
Just sittin' on the world
Tryin' to keep my feet on the ground.

I'm just sittin' on the world
And watchin' it spin
Just sittin' on the world
And tryin' hard to win.

    But I'm goin' away
    Yes, I'm leavin' today
    Yes, I'm goin' away
    'Cause there's nothin' left to say.

It's a crazy old world
As crazy as it can be
It killed the Romans once
And now it's killin' me.

I'm just sittin' on the world
Watchin' the wheels go round
Just watchin' 'em spin
until I leave this town.

    And I'm goin' a way
    Yes, I'm leavin' today
    Yes, I'm goin' away
    'Cause there's nothin' left to say.

It's a crazy old world
It's a crazy old world
It's a crazy old world

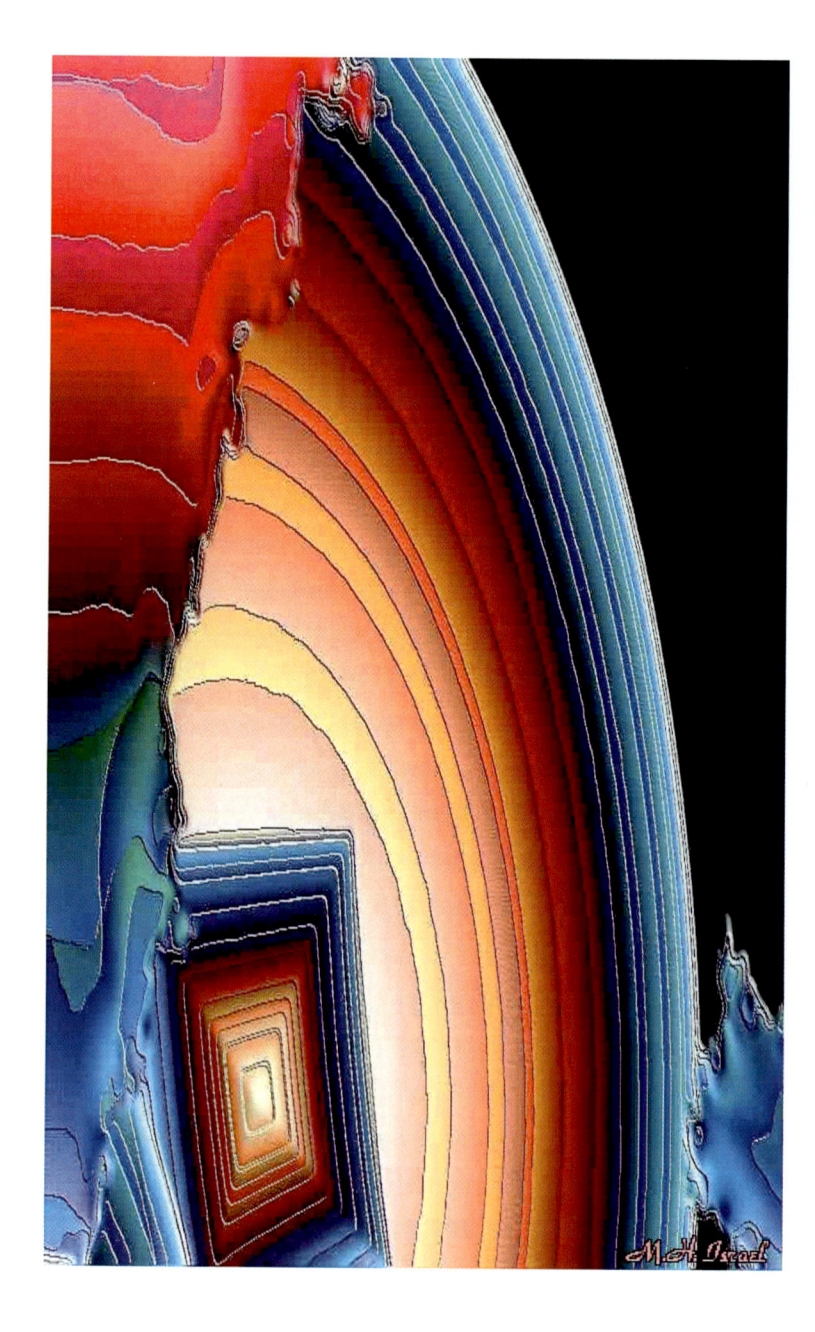

http://www.youtube.com/watch?v=bfRxohfzcxU
Search: # 74 -- "Crazy Old World" - Ukulele Man & his Prodigal Sons

Two Trees

Two trees lived in the meadow
All alone together

And they loved the world
And shared their treasures
With the boys and girls
And men and women
who passed their way.

And while the boys and girls
And men and women
Passed along their own way,

Two trees lived in the meadow
All alone together.

Wonderful Child

I used to be such a wonderful child
Where am I now?
All grown up and runnin' wild
Where am I now?

Well, I've been to the river and I've been baptized
Ate from the tree and I opened my eyes
Oh, I used to be such a wonderful child.
Where am I now?

Does it matter, do you care
That I'm getting' tattered and showin' wear
Oh, I used to be such a wonderful child.
Where am I now?

I look to see what's become of me
I don't see real clear
Look and see what's become of me
Can you help me, my Dear?

I've been to the river and I've been baptized
Ate from the tree and I opened my eyes
Oh, I used to be such a wonderful child.
Where am I now?

Where am I now?

Search: Jeff Hartley - "Wonderful Child"
http://www.youtube.com/watch?v=5KXClgerou0

Lazy Boy

My reclining chair broke his hip last week,
and being as he was old and had seen better days
that was it.
No sense in reconstructive surgery.

Tuesday he goes to the curb,
to await the undertaker,
with nothing to look forward to but
the resurrection of the upholstery.

"Remember chair that thou art dust
and to dust thou shalt return."

It hurts, what with
all those years of intimacy,
to send him away, but what could I do?

I ache, in part, because
I've become, with age, a Lazy Boy too.

Maybe when *my* hip breaks,
The kids can get another Daddy at the store
And, come Tuesday, take *me* to the curb.

Where is the Boy?

Where is the boy I used to know?
Where did he go?

Where is the boy, my old pal?
Where is he now?

Fleet of foot so quick to smile,
where is that child?

I don't know. I don't know. I miss him so.
I miss him so.

There was a time we'd walk along
Together we would sing
we would sing our song

But now he's gone and it's just me
to carry on
in a minor key

So if you see him,wish him well
Give him my love
and cast a spell

If you see him, please let him know
That I miss him and that I said "Hello."
Oh, that I said "Hello."

Where is the boy
who when work was done
sprawled on the grass
under the sun

And lying there
warmed by the sun
slipped out of time
to where all was one.

Where is the boy
who tugged on my sleeve
and drove the world away

Why did he leave?
Does he no longer believe,
no longer believe
in me?

Where is the boy, my old pal?
Where is he now?

Fleet of foot so quick to smile
where is that child?

Where is that boy who once was me?
and sat upon my Mother's knee?

There was a time we'd walk along
Together we would sing
we would sing our song

But now he's gone and it's just me
to carry on in a minor key

So if you see him
wish him well
Give him my love and cast a spell

If you see him don't say I cried
Just tell him that I love him and
that I said "Good bye"

that I said "Good bye."

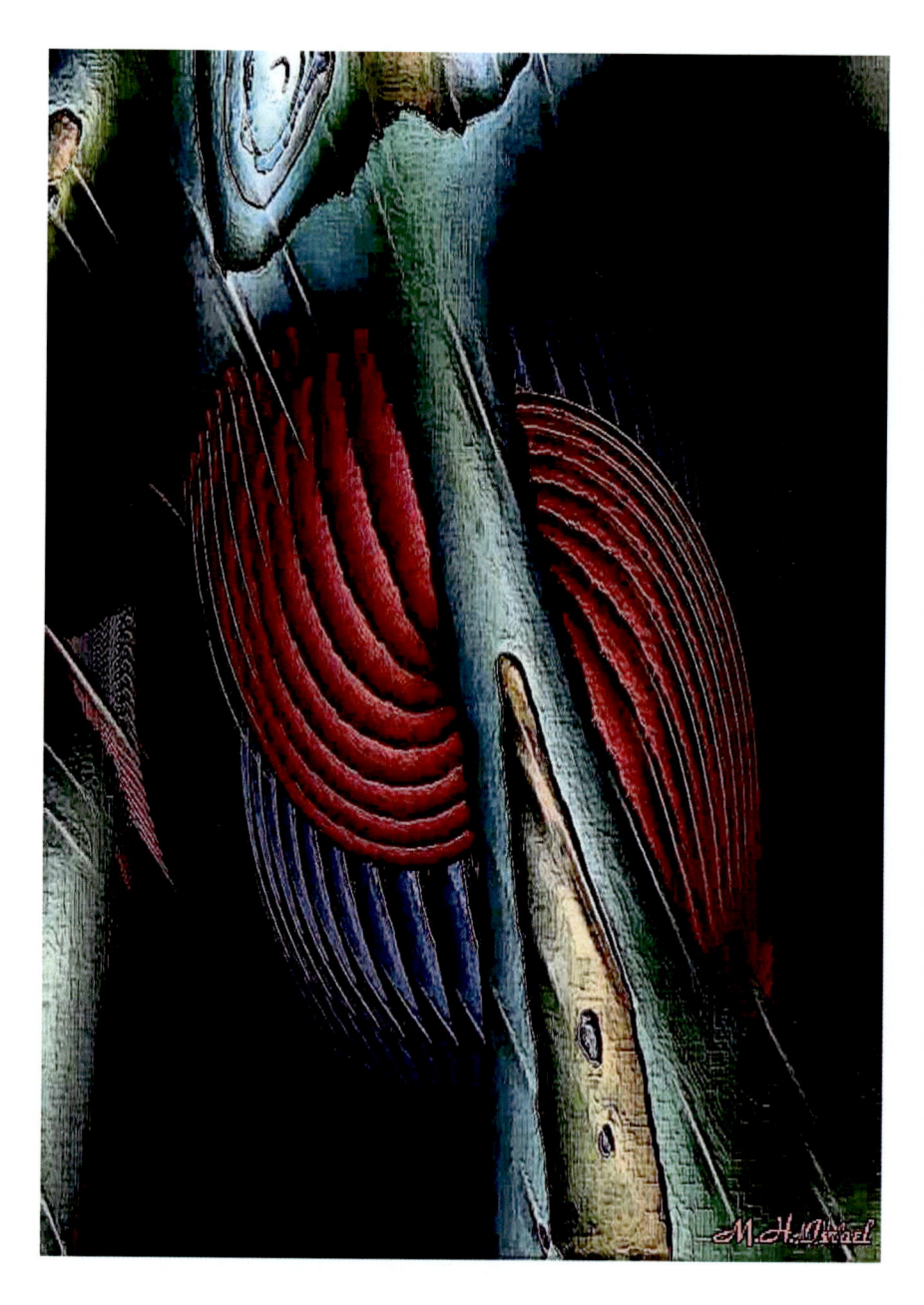

http://www.youtube.com/watch?v=AaBDJB98Djg
Search: Tom Harker # 50 - Where is the Boy

Reading Twain & Bukowski

Reading Twain & Bukowski
Reading Bukowski and Twain
I read a little bit in the morning
In the evening I read them again

Oh that's just me
Yeah that's me
Reading Twain & Bukowski

Some say Twain was a Funny Man
I say they should read him again
Some say Bukowski was a loner
Well, I say Bukowski was my friend

Oh, I knew Tom and Huckleberry
and my Barber always went to the track
I knew Sam and Henry
Some say I don't know Jack

Yeah, I can't smoke cigars like Twain
and I can't drink like a Bar Fly
but reading Twain and Bukowski
Somehow I think I'll get by

Oh that's just me
Yeah that's me
Uh huh, that's me
Reading Twain & Bukowski
Reading Twain & Bukowski
Reading Twain & Bukowski

http://www.youtube.com/watch?v=S-6edDjWqPM
Search: # 1 - Reading Twain & Bukowski

The Latest Word from Head Quarters

Life
is
a
series
of
somewhat
mistaken
notions
which
consecutively
replace
one
another
as
we
age

I Wish I Were a Pirate

I wish I were a Pirate on the Ocean
Sailing 'neath my flag of Skull & Bones
'Cause if I were a Pirate on the Ocean
Everyone would leave me all alone!!

I wish I were a Camel in the Desert
Walkin' barefoot there upon the Sand
'Cause if I were a Camel in the Desert
I'd live Alone in a Deserted Land!!

I sometimes wish that I could be a Spaceman
Floatin' through the Ozone in a Pan
'Cause if I were a Spaceman in the Ozone
I'd truly be a Solitary Man!!

I wish I were an Island in the Ocean
Complete unto myself just like a Stone
'Cause if I were an Island in the Ocean
Everyone could leave me all alone!!

I should have been a pair of Ragged Claws
Scuttling cross the floor of Silent Seas
And maybe some lost, storm-tossed Pirate
Would slow his Ship and drop a Line to me.

I should have been a Camel in the Desert
And set my Teacup there upon the Dune
And You could bring the Scones & Jam & Sugar
Pour the Tea and stir the Sugar as
We sit and sip Alone there 'neath the Moon.

Oh, I wish I were an Island in the Ocean
An Island made entirely of Stone
A Harbor for storm-tossed Pirates
A sandy Beach a Camel could call Home.

Oh, I really wish I were an Island in the Ocean
And a Pirate rode a Camel into view
Then I'd know that I could be a Spaceman
And fly into the arms of Love with You.

Then I'd know that I could be a Spaceman
And fly into the arms of Love with You.

http://www.youtube.com/watch?v=IzixKHyaqnE   Search: # 83 - Ukulele Man & his Prodigal Sons - "I Wish I Were a Pirate"

When I Die

When I die
I don't want God
there
hogging up the show

Just read from Whitman's leaves
of grass
and then
get up and go

A Tub of Buttons

I have a tub of buttons
to run my fingers through

I have a tub of buttons
Do you have some buttons too?

Q. Buttons, buttons
who's lost their buttons?

A. Those who've gone before –
I've got their history
in this tub
behind my cupboard door

    pea jackets
    little blouses
    and from off the ends of sleeves

    Time passes
    and so do we
    and this is what it leaves

    from bouncy cotton jumpers
    and yellow leisure suits
    from velvet skirts and underwear
    and Santa's special boots

    marble from the Parthenon
    leather from a goat
    plastic from recycled jugs
    anchors from a boat

    hieroglyphic messages -
    happy faces too

    You ought to have some buttons
    to run your fingers through
    Come by, and I will show you mine
    and show me yours
    please do

    before we grow much older, dear, and
    as will surely come to pass
    we lose **our** buttons too

Provincetown

Oh the sun is shinin' and the flowers are grown
Sittin' here in a cozy little home by the sea shore
By the sea shore – who could ask for anything more?

Sittin' down at the White Horse Inn
Sippin' some wine and a little bit of gin by the sea shore
Oh I could abide by the sea side

Walk down Mary Martin Avenue
Down to the bay and check out the view
Watch the cormorants glide
through the sky so wide
By the sea side

I see Jason – I see Ted
and there's Mary, just like she said
Strummin' and singin' and havin' a good time
And it don't even cost you
one thin dime
By the sea shore

You can come along
Bring your uke and sing your song
We shall while away the day
by the sea shore

Walk down Mary Martin Avenue,
Down to the bay and check out the view
Let all your cares just float away
While the colors sing and dance and play
By the sea shore

'Cause if you take your troubles down to the bay
Some sweet breeze will blow 'em away
You'll have a happy care-free sunny day
Way way out on Cape Cod bay
Where the colors sing and dance and play
By the sea shore

Oh I could abide by the sea side

http://www.youtube.com/audio?v=6xxWGfnxMCs&video_referrer=watch   Search: # 43 - Provincetown

Pogo Shtick

I know these people.
I've known them all my life.
Kiss-ups: self-serving sycophants, knee-padded beggars entreating crumbs in exchange for their honor, cowards taking the "safe" route, disgusting vermin.

I know these people.
Posers: paradigms of prodigious emptiness, icons of Warholian temporality, revered May Fly Royalty quickly caught under foot and swept away, winners at musical chairs, sad little bullet heads.

You know these people too.
You've known them all your life.
Snobs who say: "How do you like my new dress?" And "What are YOU doing here?" And "Well, I must be going now."
They say, "We run this town." And "MY son is going to PRIVATE school." And "See you at Rotary?" (do you think they wear beanies with plastic propellers there?)

You know, *snobs:*
To the manor born, stainless steel spoon in their mouths, careful parents protecting their precious ones from the "undesirable" element, on the school board so *Junior* can take the LOSING jump shot, class-conscious warriors in the classless Homeland Defense *against* "class warfare," puffed up pontificators of their own inescapable worthiness, inexhaustible exhibitionists of self-stimulation, demigods of consumption, tin pot aristocrats with streets named after them, polishing their putters and their silverware, gross toads in tiny cellars.

We know these people.
Lip-twisted Jesus-lovers spewing their racist vomit, their sexist, homophobic, parochial, creationist, censorial bile across the landscape. Moaning "persecution!" at the slightest hindrance of their self-righteous pogrom. Well-heeled healers crippling their crippled sheep during the shearing - and in turn – the carnivorous sheep, transmogrified raptors - healed and born again - return the favor to their brethren. Rendering unto Caesar. Rendering the carcass of humanity to grease the wheels of commerce. Burn the witch! Burn the Jew! Pass the plate and the ammunition too!!!

And the bullies! Pushing ahead in line, eating your lunch, establishing the pecking order (enforcers for the long term), attack dogs of the virtual reality, teacher's pets, quarterbacks, coaches, principals, cops, mayors, editors, clear-channel mouth organs, cable "news" vampires; offal, officially elected; statesmen, patriarchs, the smirking half-wit president of the US of A!!!

We know the bullies.
Home on the hill, sub-sub-sub-sub-sub-sub-suburbanites,
gated communitarians. Upper crust bluebloods, thoroughbreds. Orthodontia, acrylic nails, hair transplants, fancy pants; plastic surgeons, eggs of sturgeons; Gucci-Gucci-Gucci.

We know the bullies.
Playgrounders who steal the ball if they can't win. Self-perpetuating slackers, self-aggrandizing losers, cardboard cutouts, ostrich-eyed/bird- brained incompetents who leave their droppings where they may and delegate the clean-up.

Exploiters who bring good things to life. Engineers and oligarchs; saviors, heroes, icons; holy men and businessers, suits and CEO's.
Politicians preying and praying (with an "e"-ing and an "a"-ing). War-mongers abandoning vets - who forgive and forget (from their sick bed or their barstool) just BEFORE the *next* war.

And we know the cowards, you and I. We know them all already, know them all!! The willow reeds bending with the wind, chameleons blending in, willing wallflowers, self-deceivers, band-wagoners; toadies, informers, collaborationists, company men; narks, snitches, good soldiers, good Germans, apologists; wearers of rose-colored glasses, takers of the easy path.

Do it to Julia! Do it to Julia!   Not to me!

Windup parrots squawking of god and country, reciting the provided script, premeditatedly oblivious to hypocrisy and lies and the obvious degradation. They say, "It is our duty." "We must support our leader." "It is the white (and red and blue) man's burden!

Disgusting slugs sliming the world in their spineless, paralyzed rush to avoid being stepped upon themselves. Oh, what a well-deserved iridescent mess THAT would be, and how luminescently appropriate!

The possum warned us of these ersatz Ishmael's, riding the coffins of others to save themselves for one more day of self-delusion - these "survivors" - wrapped in the armor of self-righteous nonsense, spouting judgmental distractions, propagating emotional calluses, lips eternally puckered, shadow soldiers of the living dead struggling inch by perverted inch down the Primrose Path to the tables down at Mory's where they pass and are forgotten with the rest.

Smoking Marijuana Can Cause Mental Illness

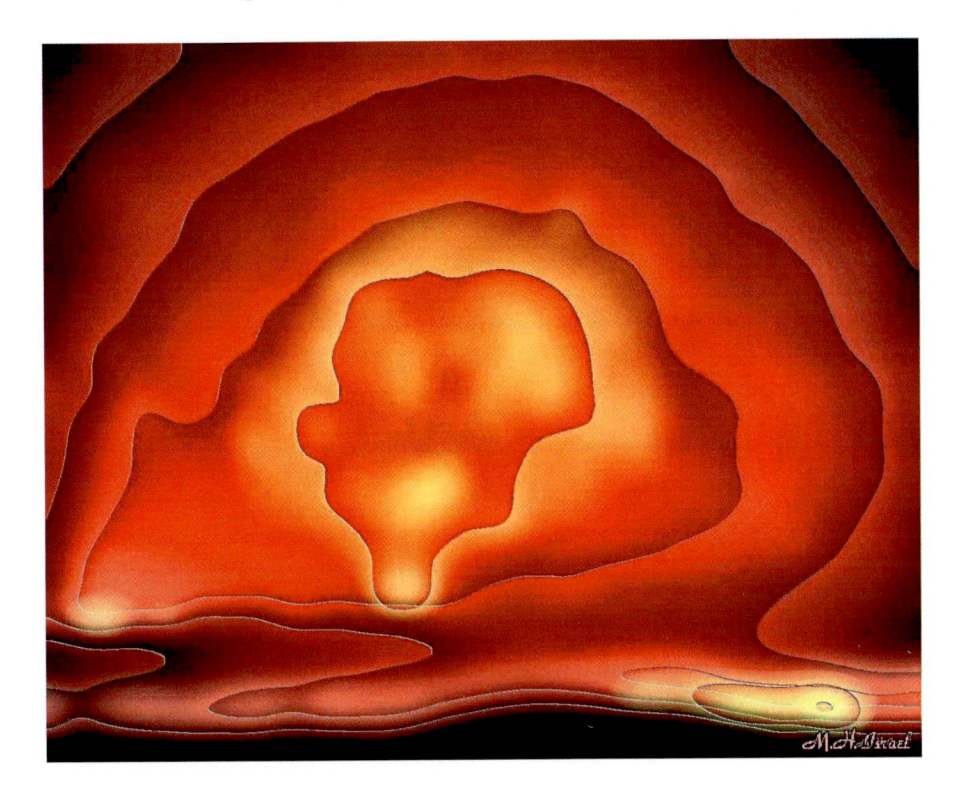

Smoking marijuana can cause mental illness
Sweating in a sauna can cause mental illness
Kissing an iguana can cause mental illness
That's why we're all insane

> Oh, the world is the insane asylum of the universe
> I'm not complaining 'cause I know it could be worse
> But we'll all still be crazy 'til they put us in the hearse
> Oh, the world is the insane asylum of the universe

Eating nuts & berries can cause mental illness
Saying your Hail Mary's can cause mental illness
Believing in Tooth Fairies can cause mental illness
That's why we're all insane

Wearing fake eyelashes can cause mental illness
Stinky cigar ashes can cause mental illness
Getting herpes rashes can cause mental illness
That's why we're all insane

Spendin' all your money can cause mental illness
Smoochin' with your honey can cause mental illness
Tellin' jokes that ain't funny can cause mental illness
That's why we're all insane

Talking on the phone can cause mental illness
Some goober's new bell-tone an cause mental illness
Listenin' t' Seline Dion can cause mental illness
That's why we're all insane

Staying out all night can cause mental illness
A missed connecting flight can cause mental illness
Drinking Bud Light can cause mental illness
That's why we're all insane

Harassment by the cops can cause mental illness
Wearing flip flops can cause mental illness
Wearing them with socks can cause mental illness
That's why we're all insane

Elvis singin' "Love Me Tender" can cause mental illness
A fielder droppin' the game ender can cause mental illness
A frog stuck in your blender can cause mental illness
That's why we're all insane

Thumping on your Bible can cause mental illness
Watching American Idol can cause mental illness
Cramps without your Midol can cause mental illness
That's why we're all insane

Cable TV rants can cause mental illness
A kitchen full of ants can cause mental illness
Playin' pool in your pants can cause mental illness
That's why we're all insane

Your pierced ear getting' torn can cause mental illness
Watchin' too much porn can cause mental illness
Even being born can cause mental illness
That's why we're all insane

There are known knowns. - Things we know we know.
There are known unknowns - We know that we don't know.
There are unknown unknowns - We don't know that we don't know,
And they *all* can cause mental illness

Oh, the world is the insane asylum of the universe
I'm not complaining 'cause I know it could be worse
But we'll all still be crazy 'til they put us in the hearse
Oh, the world is the insane asylum of the universe

Search: "Marijuana, Madness, & Donald Rumsfeld" - Ty & the Uke Man   http://www.youtube.com/watch?v=adxv7ssRegg

Where Have You Gone John Lennon ?

Where have you gone John Lennon ?
How could you leave us alone?
We'd be so glad to see you again
Please arrange if you can to come home

Where are you now, John Lennon ?
Come sit a spell next to me
Sing us a song and we'll all sing along
And again we can all feel we're free

You were my heart way back at the start
You're gone, but you're still here with me

Where have you been, John, these many long years
Have you profitably spent your time
Have you got any new songs that we can all sing
And maybe we'll find peace of mind

You were the one who made us all strong
It was you, John, who helped us keep on
And you were the one who coerced the sun
To rise up and shine down on me

But you're frozen in time now John Lennon
My heart's frozen there with you
After all of these years if you can't come to me
I guess I'll be comin' to you

So won't you come home now, John Lennon
You've been away much too long
Won't you come home, John Lennon
We've desperate need of a song

They say Lucy cried on the day that you died
And the diamonds all turned to brass
But you were my heart way back at the start
You're gone, but you're still here with me

https://www.youtube.com/watch?v=HsdljOG4DZQ   Search: # 39 - Where Have You Gone John Lennon?

Nothing Gold Can Stay

Sometimes no matter how I try
All I want to do is die.

That's when I'm tired of trying
to build a world with less of sighing
by speaking truth – instead of lying.

I am Five

Oh I am five, yes I am five
It's been five years since I arrived.
1,2,3   3,4,5
I am five, yes I am five.

Oh I am five, and my Sister's three
Yes I'm five, and my Sister's three.
She's a real cutie, just like me
I am five and my Sister's three.

Oh I am five, and my Sister's three
In two more years
she'll be as old as me
But in one more year, if I learn enough tricks,
in one more year, I'll be six.

La la la la la la la
La la la la la la la
La la la la la la la
Oh I am five, yes I am five.

Now, my Grandpa's 65
It's a wonder he is still alive
But in one more year he'll be 66
My Grandpa knows a lot of tricks

Oh I am five, yes I am five
It's been five years since I arrived
But in one more year
if I learn enough tricks
in one more year, I'll be six

1,2,3   3,4,5,6
in one more year, I'll be six
1,2,3   3,4,5,6
I'll learn some tricks
Then I'll be siiiiiiiiiiiiiiiiiiiiiiiiiiiiiiiiiiiiiiix

http://www.youtube.com/watch?v=wplpWDOWgkI
Search: Ty & the Uke Man - a 6 song - "I am Five"

My Little One

Go to sleep, my Little One
Day is almost done, my Little One

As Night must overtake the Day
Repose will surely overtake our play

Go to sleep, my Little One
And dream of things, of things yet to be

The Sun is disappearing in the West
Rest your tired cheek upon my chest

While the Moon looks down at us from candied skies
And drops his sleepy sand into your eyes

Go to sleep, my Little One
And dream of things, of things yet to be

I'll hold you in my arms, my Little One
Safe from every harm, my Little One

And someday when at last we two must part
Then you can dream and hold **me** in your heart

Go to sleep, my Little One
May lace-winged Fairies attend to thee

Go to sleep, my Little One, my Little One
And dream a World, a World as it should be be

Go to sleep, go to sleep, my Little One.

http://www.youtube.com/watch?v=xzjZwLlbpTc   Search: # 92 'Go To Sleep My Little One'

Let's Build a Mountain

Oh, the city that I live in is pretty much flat
And the white-bread boys who run it all wear a business hat
They live out in the suburbs with their barbecue
Secure in their absence from me and you

So, we gotta build a mountain
If we're to have a view
So, let's build a mountain, me and you

Oh, the city that I live in tries hard to be bland
To flatten the irregular and keep us well in hand
Smooth vanilla ice cream, oh, please no nuts
And if we don't like it, their cops'll kick our butts

So, we gotta build a mountain
If we're to have a view
So, let's build a mountain, me and you

Our aristocratic Titans wear Armani and silk
And they want us low and standardized
like homogenized milk
The Chamber likes the towers it's already got
"Oh, we don't need a mountain," says the Chamber Pot

So, we've got to build a mountain if we're to have a view
Let's build a mountain, me and you

They look out of their offices, way up in the blue
If we could build a mountain, we could be up there too
They look down their noses at us, my friend
But if we could build a mountain, we could look down on them

So, we've got to build a mountain if we're to have a view
Let's build a mountain, me and you
Oh, let's build a mountain, me and you

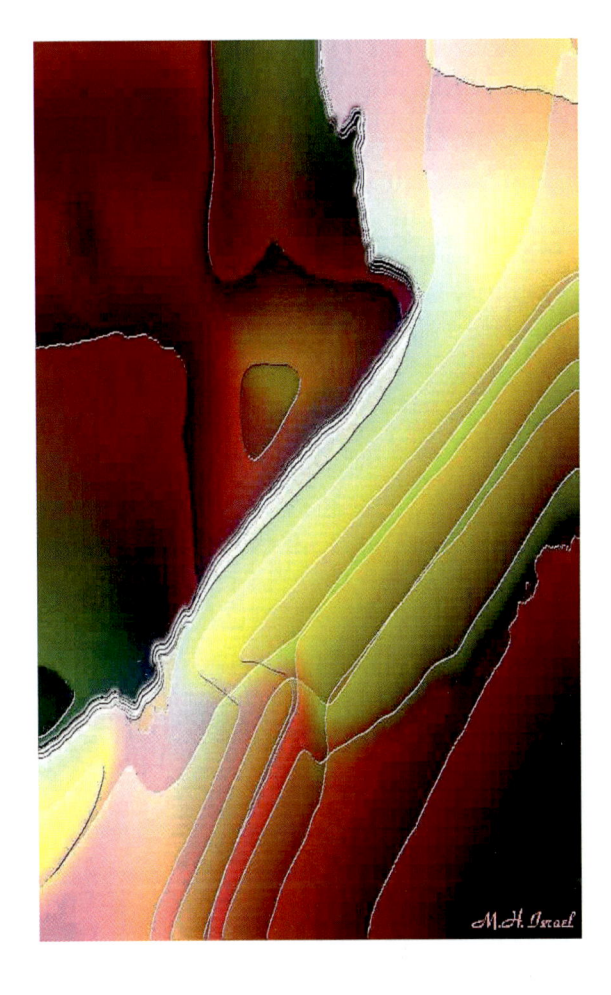

http://www.youtube.com/watch?v=Jpc9cpn-weE
Search: #70 - "Let's Build a Mountain" Uke Man Feb 3 2010

Union Maid

There once was a union maid
Who plied the Teacher Trade
She taught the three R's and stayed out o' bars
And the School Board said that she had it made

But when bargaining came around
And they tried to put her down
She held her ground with a dignified frown
And this is what she'd say

Oh, you can't scare me, I'm sticking to the union
I'm sticking to the union, I'm sticking to the union
Oh, you can't scare me, I'm sticking to the union
I'm sticking to the union 'til the day I die

This union maid was wise
To the tricks of School Board spies
She'd run 'em up a tree with a ULP
She wasn't afraid to look 'em in the eyes

And when bargaining came around
And they tried to put her down
She held her ground with a dignified frown
And this is what she'd say

Oh no, you can't scare me, I'm sticking to the union
I'm sticking to the union, I'm sticking to the union
Oh, you can't scare me, I'm sticking to the union
I'm sticking to the union 'til the day I die
I'm sticking to the union 'til the day I die

http://www.youtube.com/watch?v=KJNgDlvJxFY
Search: Ty & the Uke Man - "Union Maid"

Intelligent Design

Ah! Humanity!! God's little toy!!
His guilty pleasure; His most treasured joy!
Five days of plotting to prepare man a place
Five days of practice and wiping His face
and guzzling coffee to . . .
      what could it hurt

    to create his darling
      entirely of dirt.

Holy Roller Polka

Well, you can't be a Holy Roller if you're rollin' in the hay
Gotta thump upon your Bible, gotta thump it every day
You can't be a Holy Roller, 'less you walk the narrow way
You can't be a Holy Roller if you're rollin' in the hay

But you can be a Holy Roller and vote for David Duke
You can be a Holy Roller and be a wild-eyed kook
You can be a Holy Roller if Limbaugh is your man
You can be a Holy Roller and a wizard in the Ku Klux Klan

But you can't be a Holy Roller if you drink or smoke or chew
You can't be a Holy Roller if you like to play cards or screw
But you can be a Holy Roller – do what TV evangelists do
You can drink & smoke & chew & screw if nobody's watchin' you

So, I'm gonna be a Holy Roller. I know it will be hard
I'm gonna be a Holy Roller and get myself straight with God
I'm gonna be a Holy Roller; I really hope I can
'Cause I wantta be a Holy Roller and a wizard in the Ku Klux Klan
An' a wizard in the Ku Klux Klan, and a wizard in the Ku Klux Klan

Oh, do the Holy Roller Polka as you dance around the floor
Find someone to kick and give 'em "what for"
Find someone to blame your sins on then kick 'em some more
Do the Holy Roller Polka and march right out the door
There ain't nobody keepin' score
Do the Hooooly Rollllller Polkaaaaaaaa

http://www.youtube.com/watch?v=7BXQHNOajGw
Search # 10 - Holy Roller Polka

Monologue

So much pain

And no one is listening
Too much pain to listen

Leave me alone!

But you won't
You keep talking
You keep screaming

Shut up !

No one is listening
No one wants to listen
Can't you hear me?

I'm screaming !

Pigs

Feral pigs wander
regularly past my house.

They avoid my sight
but I sometimes hear them

high-pitched oinkers, mostly.
A few are more guttural,
usually around closing time.

And they leave their droppings for me.

Empty cigarette packs, Wendy's bags,
candy wrappers, broken beer bottles,
and half-full cans of Dew.

Too bad I live in town,
or I could shoot 'em
and make some bacon.

Stagecoach BBQ Jingle

Well, get on your horse and follow me
To South Bloomfield there on 23

There's some nice folks waitin' there for you
At the Stagecoach Barbecue.

They got slow-smoked brisket,
ribs, and pulled pork
Juicy and tender, cut it with a fork

They've got fried green beans and Grandma's Slaw
Cornbread and greens and a whole lot more

There in South Bloomfield waitin' for you
At the Stagecoach Barbecue

Oh, they're SMOKIN' !!!!

At the Stagecoach Barbecue.

    http://www.youtube.com/watch?v=ywcSlDlaD3w
    Search: the Stagecoach BBQ burned April 29, 2008

Empire

Death and destruction
are under construction.

The obligation
of this Great Nation

quite clearly, then,
is obfuscation.

    * * *

    Attention!!!

    * * *

You are approaching the end
of the moving sidewalk.

Watch your step . . .
as you leave the moving sidewalk.

Mississippi River

Sittin' down by the Mississippi River with the one I love
Thankin' God for sendin' her down for me to love

I'm so glad she calls me Dad, but I'm her little boy
Sittin' down by the river really is a joy

Sittin' down by the Mississippi River holdin' her little hand
Tellin' her that she's my girl; listenin' to her tell me I'm her man

I'm so happy she calls me Pappy, but she's my Honey Child
Sittin' down by the River really drives me wild

Sittin' down by the Mississippi River on the levy with you
I'm about out of things to say, but I know you'll show me what to do

I'm ecstatic that my erratic behavior makes you laugh
Sittin' down by the River neckin' like a giraffe

Sittin' down by the Mississippi River with the one I love
Thankin' God for sendin' her down from up above for me to love

I'm so happy she calls me Pappy, but she's my Honey Child
Sittin' down by the River really drives me wild

Oh yeah

Sittin' down by the Mississippi River with you

Search: # 81 Mississippi River
http://www.youtube.com/watch?v=FW79vEahsYo

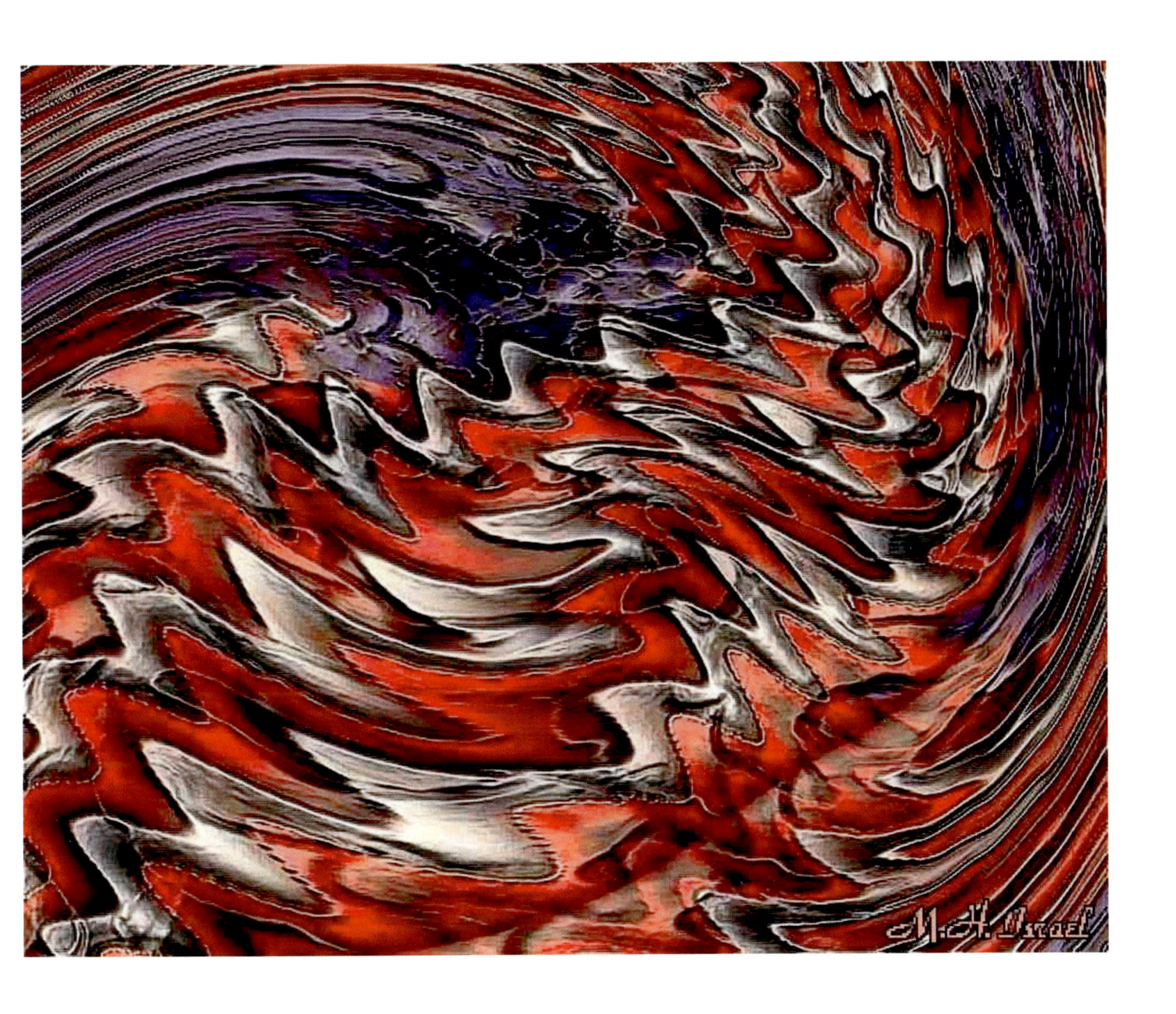

Uncle Sam's Lament

Sometimes I wake up in the mornin'
and I don't know who I am
Then my grinning nephews all rush in
saying, "Good morning, Uncle Sam"

Then they all gather round me
and they play their fifes and drum
And we all sing "God Bless America
Screw All the Other Scum"

Oh, sometimes I wake up in the mornin'
with all this money in my hand
And there's all these gold-toothed financiers
screaming, "Sam, you're the Man"

Then I go out and read the paper
and check out the 4th Estate
And read all the news that's fit to print
and everything's just great.

Then I go out and take a walk
and make my way downtown
And feel all the suspicious glances
of faces black and brown

And I don't think that they like me much
Oh, not the way they should
Can't they get it through their heads
that what I do is for their own good

This land ain't their land. This land is my land
From the Wall Street Canyons to the Silicon Valley
From Alaskan beaches to the Rio Grande
This land was made for the Man

Sometimes I wake up in the mornin'
and I don't know who I am
Then my pin-striped nephews all rush in
saying, "Get up and get at it, Uncle Sam"

Then they all gather round me
and they play their fifes and drum
And we all sing "God Bless America
Land of the Dollar & the Gun"

http://www.youtube.com/watch?v=UGuIPrQw2WI
Search: Ty & the Uke Man - "Uncle Sam's Lament"

Karl Rove

Karl Rove, poor baby
always the Doughboy
overcooked
by the redneck Texas sun

The cheating high school Debate King
looking for love in all the dark places
Master Debater over all in his way
No reality-based community for him

not **him** on his way to Empire

but, alas,
having passed his expiration date
he popped his cardboard world
on the way to the Forum

and with his doughiness exposed
was slowly devoured by a
Fox.

You Want to Take Me On

You want to take me on
You want to take me on
Well, take me on, but you'll lose

You want to turn away
Avert your eyes
Well, turn away, but you'll lose

We're all in this together
Forgetting me won't
bring you sunny weather

Take me on, turn away
forget me, but you'll lose

We're all in the same boat
If you are to survive, I too must float
Take me on, turn away
Waive the rules, and you'll lose

You want to silence me
pervert the truth
Well, silence me, but you'll lose

I'm black and white, I'm brown, I'm yellow
You can't deny that I am your fellow
Take me on, turn away
forget me, but you'll lose

Take me on, turn away
Murder me

but you'll lose

http://www.youtube.com/watch?v=5cvcVhXpHE4&feature=youtu.be
Search: # 104 - You Want to Take Me On

Moby Dick

Well, come along friends and I'll tell you the tale
Of how we took on the Great White Whale
We cut off his blubber and hauled his butt away

   And we boiled and boiled and boiled it down
   And took what's left of it to town
   And sold it to any body who'd buy the stuff
   (that's what we did, yeah)

   We boiled and boiled and boiled that stuff
   Moby Dick thought he was mighty tough
   But he'd never met up with folks like us before

He had great big teeth as big as your arm
And his body was bigger than my uncle's farm
But we cut him all up and hauled him away

He had great big bones from his tail to his head
At least the sucker did until he was dead
And we cut 'em all up and made dominoes out of them

But eternal vigilance is the price you pay
You gotta look out for Moby Dick every day
'Cause he'll be back tryin' to take a bite outta you
But if he does, well . . .

   You boil and boil and boil him down
   And take what's left of him to town
   And sell it to any body who'll buy the stuff

(that's what you do, yeah)
Boil and boil and boil that stuff
Moby Dick thought he was mighty tough
But he'd never met up with folks like us before

He's got great big teeth as big as your arm
And his body is bigger than my uncle's farm
But we cut him all up and hauled him away
Yeah, we cut him all up and hauled him away

http://www.youtube.com/watch?v=P161jRbymdg
Search: # 57 - Moby Dick (or The Negotiations Blues)

Mending Wall

We are a mighty, massive wall
That stands against the sea

You are the solid, granite blocks
The mortar joints are me

The more you press upon me, dear
The more I pull you near

Such loving reciprocity
Protects us from our fear

Yet should you press me less, old girl
Or I relax my hold

Perhaps the sea *could* make inroads
. . . If she be so bold

So press me hard, my heavy love
And I will hold you tight

We may be breached before the dawn
But not without a fight

Everyday Low Prices at Wal Mart

Long ago (much more than 7 thousand years ago)
billions of years ago actually (although it's just a theory
whose opponents know [for a certainty]
how many angels can dance on the head of a pin)

elemental bits of happenstance and serendipity
were consumed in the bowels of the earth and
(egged on by gravitational passion)
consummated their periodic elemental coitus.

Pricked on against rest
(by overwhelming inertia) and
blessed by the limitless permutations of time,
gestation (eventually) brought forth
primordial Ooze

from the crack of the Mother
earth

and it ate its insensitive elemental brethren
(which was no bother to anyone)
and eventually

(consumed by passion)

foolishly Knew itself
(though a child at heart)
and complicated things further

And

with knowledge
complications geometrically progressed

until

All ate each other
(brothers, sisters, parents, and children)
All & None: innocent
All & None: guilty

Consuming, consummating, and consumed

Etcetera

FINALLY

(we would like to say)

WE (upright folks that we are) appeared on the shelf
to be Known and to Know.

NEW & IMPROVED
(the best yet)
(god's pet)
(no longer wet
behind the ears)

Dedicated
to consume and be consumed
in the Ultimate consummation
of our carnival knowledge

and to put an end
to this Mobius trip.

So

Eat me sister
and I'll eat you
and let us consummate our complications
so that What (we do not know)
shall (blessed by the permutations of time)
carry on (perhaps)

the splendor of
the consumer.

Everyday low prices at Wal-Mart

A Broom and a Wastebasket

There's a man on the floor
in front of the restroom
at the bus terminal
of the Port Authority
on my way to Passaic

he's not moving.

I told a cleaning lady who passed by
with a broom and a wastebasket

I told her

There's a man on the floor
in front of the restroom
at the bus terminal
of the Port Authority
on my way to Passaic

he's not moving.

Barnyard in the Sky

Oh, the pigs they've got religion
They worship Farmer Brown
Services each morning
When he brings their slop around

They all keep the faith
'Cause they know that when they die
They're goin' to that Great Big Happy
Pig Stye in the sky

    "Good ol' Farmer Brown
    He never lets us down
    Always brings our slop around
    He should wear a crown
    That good ol' Farmer Brown"

And the chickens watch their language
In front of their chicks
Don't want to warp their little minds
Talkin' politics

They hear the preachin' Parrot
What lives in the house
Preachin' long-sufferin' humility
An' t'be quiet as a mouse

And they've all got religion
'Cause they know that when they die
They're goin' to that Happy
Chicken Coop up in the sky.

And every now and then
Good ol' Farmer Brown
Takes a load of animals
For a ride into town

To those greener pastures
Where he lays them down
And with a lovely crimson hue
They get to paint the town

> "Good ol' Farmer Brown
> He never lets us down
> He always wears a smile
> You'll never see a frown
> When he gets back from town
> That good ol' Farmer Brown"

And should the grizzled donkey
Dare express his doubts
About his missing friends
And their actual whereabouts

The sheep will surround him
And bleat into his face
that their missing brethren
Are in a better place

And they've all got religion
'Cause they know that Farmer Brown
On some fine day to come
Will choose *them* to take to town

To those greener pastures
Where he'll lay them down
And with a lovely crimson hue
They too can paint the town

"Good ol' Farmer Brown
Good ol' Farmer Brown
I know someday he'll take
Every one of us to town
An' bye and bye we're gonna fly
To that Happy Barnyard in the Sky

You an' me and Good Ol' Farmer Brown"

http://www.youtube.com/watch?v=jRacKOUMJD4   Search: # 69 - Ukulele Man: "ANIMAL FARM - Barnyard in the Sky"

When I Write a Song

When I write a song
I make a baby.

Blind coitus
Plants a seed
And nothing can stop gestation.

This and that
And other things
Go on for months,
But baby grows, and stretches,
Grows, and kicks
Then sucks her thumb
Awhile.

In time, squash-faced and squalling,
And beautiful to me,
She's here
Not completely formed

But in time,
And dressed in tuneful clothes,
What a joy she is.

So sweet
With her wide eyes
And chubby cheeks.

Want to see her picture?

Headin' for the Moon

I'm flyin' in the sky - flyin' o'er the clouds - headin' for the Moon
I'm flyin' in the sky -   flyin' o'er the clouds - headin' for the Moon
I just saw a cow go by – a cow jumped over the Moon
The little dog laughed to see such sport
And I ate my cereal with my spooooon

    The Man in the Moon is a Custard Pie
    Hangin' way up in the sky
    And I'll get there too bye & bye – you'll see
    'cause I'm flyin' in the sky - flyin' o'er the clouds - headin' for the Moon

I'm ridin' in my train – ridin' cross the Plains – headin' for the Moon
I'm ridin' in my train – ridin' cross the Plains – headin' for the Moon
Hey!! a buffalo just flew by – buffalo flew over the Moon
The little dog laughed to see buffalo wings
And I ate my cereal with my spooooon

The Man in the Moon is a Custard Pie
    Hangin' way up in the sky
    And I'll get there bye & bye – you'll see
    'cause I'm flyin' in the sky - flyin' o'er the clouds - headin' for the Moon

I'm lookin' out my window - lookin' up my tree - headin' for the Moon
I'm climbin' out my window - climbin' up my tree - headin' for the Moon
And Little Jack just climbed by – Jack climbed over the Moon
The Giant didn't like it much
but I bonked him on the noggin' with my cereal spoon

The Man in the Moon is a Custard Pie
    Hangin' way up in the sky
    And I'll get there bye & bye – you'll see
    'cause I'm flyin' in the sky - flyin' o'er the clouds - headin' for the Moon

    But then, the Man in the Moon looked out of the Moon
    Looked out of the Moon and said
    You can't come up here with me
    'Cause you've gotta go to bed !!

    But the Man in the Moon is nothin' but a silly Custard Pie
    So I ate him all up with my cereal spoon
    And then just waved bye-bye !!

And I'm flyin' in the sky - flyin' o'er the clouds - headin' for the Moon
I'm flyin' in the sky - flyin' o'er the clouds - headin' for the Moon
Headin' for the Moon

http://www.youtube.com/watch?v=sAA1WcQ_brc   Search: Ukulele Man - "Headin' for the Moon"

Yo Soy Abuelo

Yo soy Abuelo
No tengo pelo
Pero vuelo en el cielo
con Paloma

Yo soy Abuelo
No tengo dinero
Pero vuelo en el cielo
con Paloma

>Abrimos nuestros brazos y
>llegan a ser alas
>y hacemos la magia
>Paloma y Abuelo
>
>Gorjear elevamos
>Una vez más soy joven
>en los ojos brillantes
>de Paloma
>
>¿Es tu abuelo tan loco?
>Bien, quizás un poco
>Pero vuelo en el cielo con Paloma
>
>¿Es Paloma tan chistosa ?
>No, pero Abuelo será pronto
>cuándo vuelo en el cielo con Paloma

Yo soy Abuelo
No tengo pelo
Pero tengo mi nieta hermosa

Yo soy Abuelo
No tengo dinero
Pero tengo mi querida, Palomita

Vuelo por el cielo   Encima de las nubes   Bajo un sol sonriente

Abuelo vuela al cielo con Paloma

http://www.youtube.com/watch?v=TYHxj9YionU

Search: # 101 Paloma's Song

My Name is Frances

My name is Frances – I'm a fancy pants-es
I do all the dances when my Grandpa plays and sings

My name is Frances – I'm a fancy pants-es
I can dance and do most anything !!

I had a banana with my Nana
I had grilled-cheese with Aunt Louise
I had some peanut butter with Audrey's little brother
Can I have my cookie now, please?

My name is Frances – I'm a fancy pants
You can be a fancy pants, too
Come join the dance - Jump, sing, and prance
While Grandpa sings and plays his uke for you

I see London, I see France, putting on their fancy pants
When Frankie says, "It's time to dance!!"
Stamps her foot and gives a glance

Gigglin' and bubblin', it's time, she knows
To dance the dance, the fancy dance
The magical dance of the Fancy Pants

My name is Frances – I'm a fancy pants-es
I do all the dances when my Grandpa plays and sings

My name is Frances – I'm a fancy pants-es
I can do almost anything !!
I can do almost anything !!

http://www.youtube.com/watch?v=BkzlI7nOw4s
Search: # 89 My Name is Frances

I'm Gwendolyn Josephine

I'm Gwendolyn Josephine, but you can call me Jo-Jo
I can get around – I'm always on the go, you know
I'm Gwendolyn Josephine, but you can call me Jo-Jo
I've always got a smile, I'm such a sweet child, and a grumpy lip's a no-no

And I like to hear my Grandpa play on his You-Koo-Lay Lay Lay Lay Lay
And when he sings and whistles and whoots
It's time to put on my Jo-Jo Go-Go Boots

Got my MoJo workin'
Got my Grandpa to play
Got my dancin' boots on
Don't get in my way

And when Grandpa starts to play
My go go boots show the way
To swing and sway the day away
The happy Jo-Jo Go-Go way

She's got her MoJo workin'
Workin' all day
And Joey can dance
As long as Grandpa can play

She' Gwendolyn Josephine but I can call her Jo-Jo
She can get around – she's always on the go, you know
She's Gwendolyn Josephine but I can call her Jo-Jo
She's always got a smile – she's such a sweet child
and Grandpa ought to know!!!

http://www.youtube.com/watch?v=w2yQoTWpRBk
Search: # 91 I'm Gwendolyn Josephine

Rich

There he goes, Rich's on his way
The strong, silent type - doesn't have a lot to say

Stronger than Superman, tougher than ol' King Kong
And if you slip him a blueberry, he'll take you along

There he goes, openin' up a door
Now he's closin' it so it's just like it was before

He knows how it goes, but watch out for your fingers and toes
Who knows when he'll strike again? Richie's quite the man!!

Here he comes to sit on Grandpa's knee
Climbs up like Spiderman and gives a hug to me

I give one back to him as fast as I can
Grandpa loves a hug from his little Tarzan

http://www.youtube.com/watch?v=f7C19DBf-l4
Search: # 110 - Rich

Oh, A. J.

Oh A.J., come sit on Grandpa's knee
I'll give you a hug & you can give one back to me
Oh A.J., come sit on Grandpa's knee
I'll give you a kiss & you can give it back to me.

Oh A.J. you're such a happy child
sparkling bright eyes and a happy little smile.
Oh A.J. let me see that smile,
and Grandpa will be happy all the while.

Oh A.J., come take Grandpa's hand
Together we can walk through Childhood's magic land.
I'll bring my ukulele and sing a happy tune
About Grandpa and A.J. and the Man in the Moon

Oh A.J., come sit on Grandpa's knee
I'll give you a hug & you can give one back to me
Oh A.J., come sit on Grandpa's knee
I'll give you a kiss & you can give it back to me

http://www.youtube.com/watch?v=ji73utm_uNM&feature=youtu.be
Search: # 109 - Oh A J

Out Out

I killed a cat last night
in the late dusk near the end of May.

It was a brindle cat
that galloped with a wobble
across State Route 23.

I swerved but it didn't help.

Thud-ump

and that was it.

Nothing to build on there.
So I - since I was not the one dead -
went about my business.

But the cat came with me.

She's with me still,
 a reminder,
(like Saddam Hussein and Joan of Arc)
of the sudden stop –

nine lives notwithstanding.

Together on the Sand

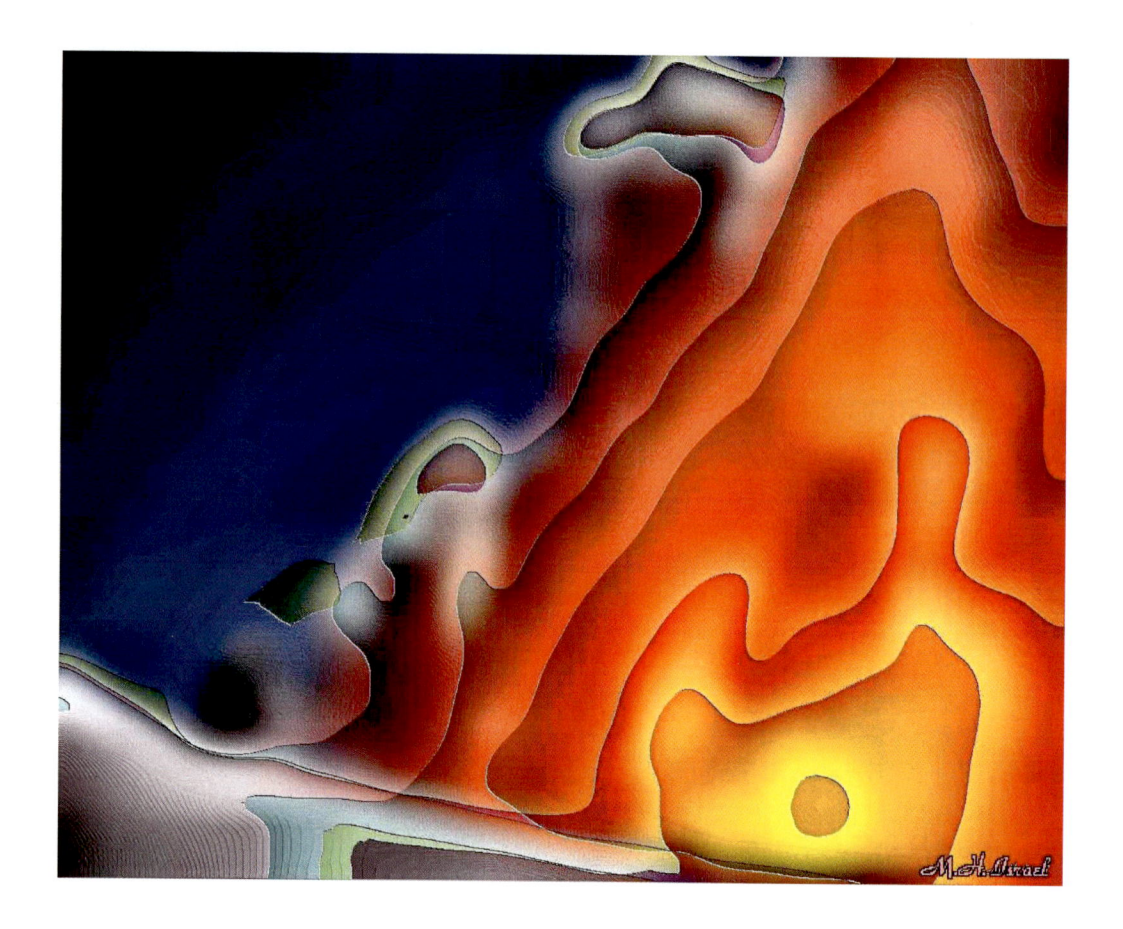

Why don't we go you and me
Down to the ocean and see what we can see
Walkin' there together on the sand

Why don't we take a moment for ourselves
And see where that moment goes
Siftin' the beach between our toes

Nobody knows what tomorrow may bring
But as long as we can sit there and sing
I won't worry 'bout a thing
long as you are there with me

We can sit and gaze out at the sky
And at the sea you and I
Oh wouldn't that be grand
Sittin' there together on the sand

Nobody knows what tomorrow may bring
But as long as we can sit there and sing
I won't worry 'bout a thing,
long as you are there with me

Why don't we go you and me
Down to the ocean and see what we can see
Walkin' there together on the sand

Walkin' there together hand in hand

http://www.youtube.com/watch?v=TcW3JNHM3Ak
Search: # 67 - "Walking There Together on the Sand"

1999

At the hospital
I helped Mom down the long hallway
to the last room at the end.

"The Price Is Right!" was on
and Uncle Joe was the next contestant.

He didn't hear our
hello's
so I began to peel an orange
for the rest of us.

Just then
(before Bob Barker was ready)
Uncle Joe selected
the Showcase behind the final curtain
and left us there alone . . .

waiting for Don Pardo
to tell us what he'd won.

Goin' Home

I'm goin' home, I'm outta here
But I could stick around for maybe one more beer
I'm goin' home, leavin' today
And I'll get there though there's hell to pay

I'm goin' home, yeah, I've done my time
I've sung my song I've made my rhyme
I'm goin' home, nothin' left to say
I'm goin' home, no more gigs to play

    And I've done everything I could
    To live life like they said I should
    And I guess it's true what they say about me
    My days are through, but I don't care any more

Yeah, I'm goin' home, had enough of this
But I wouldn't mind just one more kiss
So, hold me, Babe, but don't you cry
I just stopped in to say "Goodbye"

I'm goin' home, had enough of this world
I won't miss much, but I'll miss you girl
I'm goin' home, had enough of this place
I'm goin' home but I'll miss your face

    And I've done everything I can
    To live life like a man
    But I guess it's true what they say about me
    My days are through, and I don't care any more

Yeah, I'm goin' home, yeah my days are through
Don't mourn for me, find someone new
I'm goin' home, don't you be blue
Don't cry for me; I'll cry for you

    And I've done everything I could
    To live life like they said I should
    And I guess it's true what they say about me
    My days are through, but I don't care any more

And I no longer wonder where I'm bound

http://www.youtube.com/watch?v=vx_Dc5jb5XU
Search: # 106 - I'm Goin' Home

Life in the Garden

Man is brother to the Radish

a hardy seed of promise
planted in the dark and sprouting there
to push, in time, his tiny, shiny ears
into the Light
where he listens and
imperceptibly
grows
into the strangeness of the day and
the conundrum of the night.

The little fellow, cute and plump,
but tender still, all agog with wonder,
in time gives way to teen,
dancing in delirium, oblivious of oblivion.

Then, the proud Adult,
muscular citizen
contributing to his nation
and ready to enlist in the Greengrocer Wars.

Those that survive drought and disease
and the cold hand of the Market,
soon droop and thicken
wearing the scars of their passage,
the wages of their struggle.

Inevitably, though,
grim Jack appears and with his icy breath
collects the rent.

Rot is his receipt.

In the end
naught is left but brittle bones,
pale husks of once robust stems,
venerable relics
mourned by a hundred hardy seeds of promise,

hopeful progeny
awaiting their own awakening.

Flowers

There upon the hill I found my Daffodil
So young and so demure, so sweet and pure

Oh, the hours I've spent with flowers
Have changed my attitude, made me less rude
Left me in a mood

Oh, my lovely Lilac
in May you're in full bloom
You captured me with your lush perfume

Oh, the hours I've spent with flowers
Have changed my attitude, made me less rude
Left me in a mood

A bed of roses, some might wish
Or Gardenias floating in a dish
But pray your wishes meet your needs

Remember: Flowers bloom among the weeds

And the hours I've spent with flowers
Have changed my attitude, made me less rude
Left me in a mood

Oh, Tulips pressed to mine
I drink a heady wine
Burgundy and Cabernet
You take my breath away

And the hours I've spent with flowers
Have changed my attitude, made me less rude
Left me in a mood

Oh, the hours I've spent with flowers
Have pulled me through

http://www.youtube.com/watch?v=e7gmeqKBDwY
Search: # 11 - The Hours I've Spent with Flowers

You Are My Sunshine

Did you know that
some days the sun shines
and warms the meadow,
while all the while projecting
sub-atomic particles of darkness –

subliminal shade.

You cannot see them,
these particles;
they're much too small,
but in time they'll clot
to lumps and threads,

spidery webs
that cast faint shadows
on the grass.

But that's not all,

for the flypaper strands
entrap the lurking blackness
in every nascent sunbeam,
enwrap themselves
again, and again;
and thicken.

Threads become ropes,

the web a net,

an expanding net of shrinking windows,

shrinking, shrinking, shrinking!
Until they are shut – Tight!
by pulsing woof and warp,

and all is dark.

Then I beat my head upon the ground
Until I can see the stars.

Sunny day in Baghdad

Another sunny day in Baghdad,
Just another sunny day in Baghdad,
Mowing sand and slowly goin' mad
It's another sunny day in Baghdad,

Suni and Shii
say "Hello there G.I.
We've got a cell phone call for you."

Billy goes for a ride
Then all his buddies died
When that cell phone call came through -
It's just a local call in Baghdad.

    But everything's OK
    In our sand-trap USA
    Yes, sir!! The sun shines every day.
    It's always a sunny day
    in Baghdad,

From his stretcher Billy cried
For all his friends who had died,
And his eyes clouded up with tears,
it's true.

But in the end -
you know the drill, my friend
In Baghdad the sun always breaks through.

It's always a sunny day in Baghdad,

And everything's OK
    In our make-shift USA
        Yes, sir!! The sun shines every day.
    It's always a sunny day
    in Baghdad,

Billy pulled R&R in Germany
But I don't think he'll be writin' me
He left both his hands behind, you see.
On that sunny day in Baghdad.

But our leaders swear it's true
That we must do what we must do –
And they know so much more than
Billy, you, and me;
They've spent a sunny day in Baghdad.

And everything's OK
    In our make-shift USA
        Just mowing sand and
            slowly goin' mad.

I wrote Billy yesterday
Didn't have much to say, just
"It's another sunny day in Baghdad."

Yeah, I wrote Billy yesterday
    Didn't have much to say
Just "It's another sunny day in Baghdad."

http://www.youtube.com/watch?v=rNMIg6AR-Zo
Search: # 2 - Sunny Day in Baghdad

Our Glorious Virtual Reality

Everything depends
on everyone
pretending

that it's always been
this way
no beginning and no ending.

It's Life and Death
to those on top
not to let the
bubble
pop !

But to those down
on the
bottom,
I say,
"Smoke 'em

If you've got 'em."

Polar Bears

Out of the North come the Polar Bears
working hard, and they're looking for lard.

Some people like me are fat, you see
and we've tried every plan devised by man.
Though we wail and suffer travail,
in the end we fail to be bad to the bone,
we fail to atone, to be skin and bone.

But out of the North come the Polar Bears
working hard, and they're looking for lard.

In their eyes are Eskimo Thighs
and from their nose drips adipose.
They lick their lips when they see my hips
It's a hip reduction by lip - o - suction !

And out of the North come the Polar Bears
working hard, and they're looking for lard.

Oh Jenny Craig, there goes a leg,
oh, Slim Fast, there goes my ass.
They lick their lips when they see my hips.
It's a hip reduction by lip - o - suction !

And out of the North come the Polar Bears
working hard, and they're looking for lard.

If weight gain is causing you pain,
driving you insane,
I'm proud to announce
you can lose
every ounce
we can atone
be bad to the bone
just get on the phone
make a date with a Polar Bear !!

And out of the North come the Polar Bears
working hard, and they're looking for lard.

http://www.youtube.com/watch?v=CjaAQZr-Lhs&feature=youtu.be
Search: # 108 - Out of the North Come the Polar Bears

Graduation Day
Uke Man's Generic Small Town/Rural High School Graduation Speech*

(as inspired by the underlying, but unspoken, reality of life in the small town of Ovalville, Ohio - where I live and where you will find Ovalville High School and its Fighting Merinos).

Hey Graduates!!

Congratulations!! You made it.

Oh yes, I know that even as you wait excitedly to throw your caps into the air, you are wondering: **" Golly, what now? What lies ahead?"**

Hmmmmmmm..... Two roads diverge in a yellow wood, and I'll (yes, *I'll*) take the one less traveled by, and that'll make all the difference.

Yeah . . . uh-huh.

Well, I'm here to say, like Yogi Berra, *"If you come to a fork in the road, take it."* You see, Yogi lived on a street that forked before it reached his house, but it soon came back together. Whichever road you took, it really didn't make any difference.

It's the same for you, graduates (although most of you – not to mention your English teachers - have likely misread Frost's poem - read the poem again when you're forty, and if you're still puzzled, e-mail me).

What I mean is, everything's pretty much already been decided for you by now. And better yet, you don't really have to worry about it. **You've been to High School!!!**

Just think back! All the answers to all the major questions are there! You know where the railroad tracks are; don't you? And you know where you live; don't you? Well, that's the main thing.

That should tell you something, make my job today a lot easier, and help get your individual self on the road to adjustment and acceptance.

Now, you *losers* out there – you know who you are – you ***should,*** since you've had it hammered into your heads, probably since elementary school : "dummies, dorks, slackers, dopers, burn-outs, goths, punks, geeks, nerds, porkers, wallflowers, skanks, spastics, and speds."

Well, you're on *your* road already, and the rest of the class intends to keep you there. At least, they're not going to help you get out of that rut (yours is a tough life, but *they* insist that somebody has to live it).

Get used to it. Put your nose to the grindstone. Work hard. Save for a rainy day, take an entry level job, work your way up to cashier, and salute the flag!

No. Today I am not talking to you, you vast assemblage of losers, begrudgingly sitting out there in the sun – although I may share a few beers with you after the ceremony. You already know what you have to do: the same thing you've always had to do - for twelve years – survive! Get used to it. Embrace it. It is your ***destiny***.

Ah, but you winners!! Fear not. You have the answers; you know the rules; you *learned them in school*.

Well . . . you certainly have ***assimilated*** them, but probably you didn't actually *learn* them in any academic sense. So, just to be sure, let me enumerate them now:

Number 1. You were born to rule (remember the railroad tracks? count your dividends!).

Number 2. If challenged, point out how much better dressed and coiffed you are (let 'em deal with *that*!).

Number 3. Failing that, your parents *do* have power, money, and influence. Have them crush the upstarts.

Number 4. Never forget that the socio-economic- political system will *always* support *you* in your efforts since it is run by people who are winners too - people just like *you* !

Number 5. (To state the obvious) Intelligence, talent, insight, energy, and altruism are unnecessary – and, perhaps, even counter-productive (as everyone knows, a large portion of you cheated your way through "Honors" classes for four years and are still considered "gifted"). Dexterity and cunning uber alles!

And, last but not least, a valuable corollary: While those sitting around you have muddled through in obscurity, you've done well for yourself here, BUT: **don't over-reach!!!!**

Raised in a small, conservative, heartland environment, you probably already appreciate being a big fish in a small pond and are understandably hesitant to expose your shortcomings by trying for too much more. **Good idea!**

The bigger fish, bigger than you, know the rules too and frown on "helping the world" - even more than you do (and they consider *you* – yeah, I know that's hard to imagine -as part of "*the world*").

Now, a lot of you "gifted" folks out there may have gotten nervous and started asking yourself, *"Does this jerk really know what he's talking about?"*

Yeah, it is hard to believe. **You** know that you're not particularly special. **You** know that your parents and class-conscious teachers got you by, while the system selectively ground down the "beaners" and "sweathogs" and "hippies" and "dweebs." **You** know that you've had all the advantages that the losers lacked – through no fault of their own - that **you**'ve been arbitrarily lifted up while they've been relegated to obscurity. And you wonder if they resent you.

Of course they do, but they can't do a damn thing about it. Can they?!! Remember "THE RULES"!!! Rules are rules, and as the ruling minority you've taken the road less traveled by. It's your *job* to keep it that way.

Perhaps you find this new responsibility daunting, but don't worry. Our great democracy is based on the principle: *"You can fool all of the people some of the time, and some of the people all of the time, and - with control of the media - those are pretty good odds."*

That bedrock foundation will always sustain you. You might be - by any objective measure - an incompetent, a fool, and a failure; but with the right parents, the right attitude, the right clothing and grooming, and – perhaps – with a little golf; the system will take care of you.

You've got it made. Never forget that the world is run by pompous little self-serving bullet-headed winners - just like you - and they *won't* let you down . . . (unless they can make a few bucks out of it). Congratulations!! And *may you always get what you so richly deserve!!*

-- Thank You

* If you find this address suitable to your town (small, rural, or otherwise), I am available (fees may vary with location and the relative likelihood of facing angry mobs).

Pee Wee Where Have You Gone

Oh Pee Wee, where have you gone?
Have you run off with Miss Yvonne?
Reba Mail Lady says no forwarding address;
oh Pee Wee, we miss you I confess.

Cowboy Curtis still rides the range,
but his eyes look mighty strange.

Oh Pee Wee, won't you come home?
Chairy can't stand livin' here all alone.
We're gonna sit here every Saturday
'til you come home again to play.

Mecca lecca hi, mecca hiney ho,
mecca lecca hi, mecca hiney ho,
mecca lecca hi, mecca hiney ho,
oh oh oh oh oh - where did you go?

Did somebody say wish?

Oh Pee Wee, wish you were here,
to bring the Playhouse some cheer;
we're gonna sit here every Saturday,
'til you come home again to play. .

Mecca lecca hi, mecca hiney ho,
mecca lecca hi, mecca hiney ho,
mecca lecca hi, mecca hiney ho,
oh oh oh oh oh - where did you go?

Come back, Pee Wee

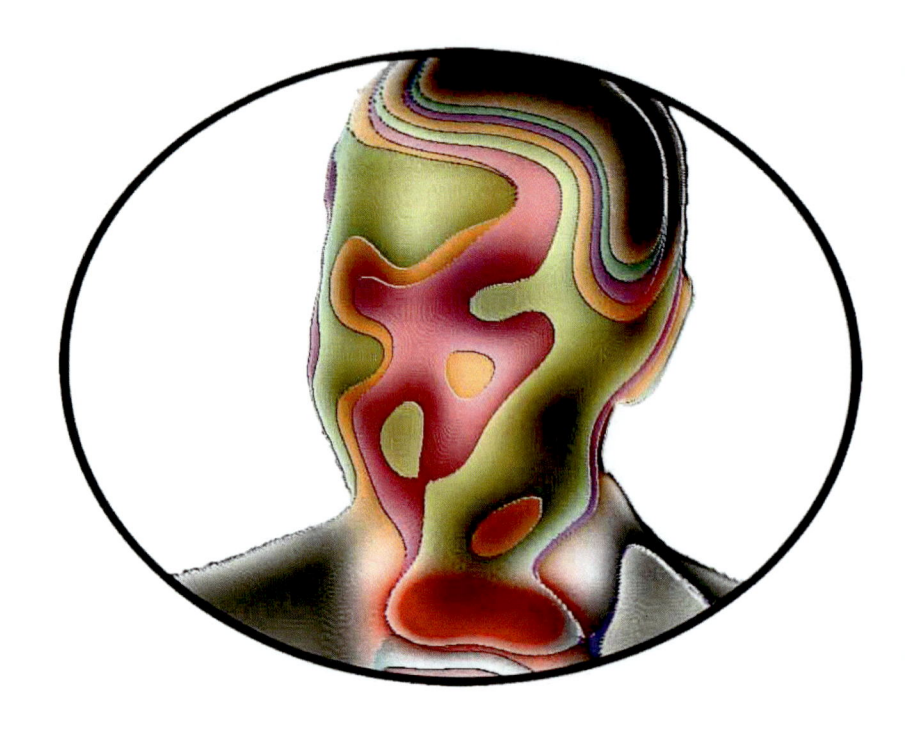

http://www.youtube.com/watch?v=i5aqb0gunaU
Search: Pee Wee Where Have You Gone

Drinking with Kermit

Once
on a very sunny day
after several bourbons
and practice runs of
"The Rainbow Connection,"
I walked out my door
into a strange world
and found myself
pushing through
a transparent gelatin of
glistening psychedelic intensity,
striding with determination
through a Wonderland bereft of meaning.

Too soon the dream
collapsed and fell away,
crushed by
the virtual reality
it had offended
and,

too soon,
propriety was restored.

To Shelley

The mystery of life escapes me
most of the time
And yet I know its tension.
I can feel it
all around,
a mystery yet reality.

It is a gift I have
to sense its existence there
around me
and around you.

It is your gift too,
to know what escapes
so many others.

I perceive your essence
and am glad.

Neither of us
is alone.

King of the World

I could have been so much more
if you had believed in me

But dreams take wing and fly away
when they cannot stay with you
I could have been so much more
if you had believed in me

I could have been king of the world
if you had just been my girl
We could have ruled wondrous lands
if you had just taken my hand

But dreams are things that slip a way
when they cannot stay with you
I could have been king of the world
if you had believed in me

I could have been a Hollywood star
if you had just said, "You'll go far"
Clark Gable would bow to me somehow
if you had just been my gal

But dreams can fade to shades of grey
when they cannot stay with you
I could have been a Hollywood star
if you had believed in me

We could have sung magical songs
if you had just sung along
But the world's not heard yet
such a lovely duet
'cause you left me standing alone

Oh dreams you see take a minor key
when they cannot be with you
I could have been king of the world
if you had believed in me

I could have been, oh, so much more
if you had believed in me

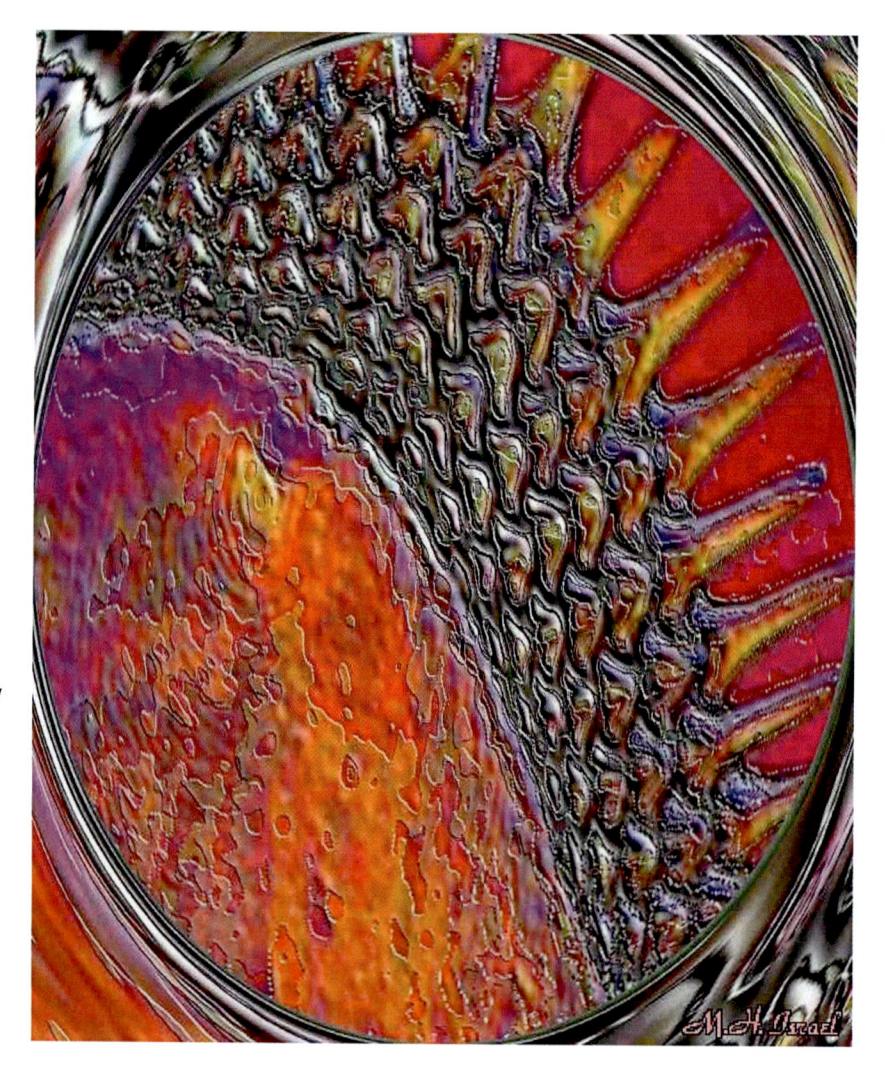

https://www.youtube.com/watch?v=dNKtwO1O8Us
Search: # 41 - Sippin' & Spittin' (King of the World)

And Now

I never did what she wanted
or maybe she never wanted what I did
or maybe when I did what she wanted
she didn't want it any more.

In any case,
I finally did whatever I did
without regard to what she wanted.

In that beginning I knew what I did
was what I wanted.
Now, I **do**,
But I don't **know**

and sometimes I don't care.

Love is Something

Love is something everybody needs
But today it's here and tomorrow it leaves
Love is something we can't count on
Today it's here – tomorrow it's gone.

Love is an ocean flowing all around
Love is a continent – feet firmly on the ground
Still, love is something we can't count on
Today it's here – tomorrow it's gone.

All you need is love – rum pa pum pa pum
All you need is love – rum pa pum pa pum
All you need is love – love – love is all you need

Love has the answers to life's questions, my friend
But when the questions keep on changing
Then love will end
Love is something we can't count on
Now you see it – and now it's gone.

All you need is love – rum pa pum pa pum
All you need is love – rum pa pum pa pum
All you need is love – love – love is all you need
Love is all you need

http://www.youtube.com/watch?v=wKxuF9cwt0k
Search: # 7 - Love Is Something

If I Love You (a duet: *m* = man – *w* = woman – **t** = together)

If I love you, would I dare
To tell you all about it
Wonderin' if you'd care ?   m

And if I love you, would it be
the start of something wonderful
or just the end of me
If I love you.

    If I love you, would I dare
    To embrace you
    And show you that I care

    If I love you, would we be
    Lovers forever   w
    Through eternity
    If I love you

        If I love you true
        Would you let me be
        a part of you   **t**
        Or would it simply be
        The end of me
         If I love you

Yes, I love you, I truly do
And I'm so much more a man   m
for being part of you.

    Yes I love you, my love is true
    Together we can face the world   w
    and see it through
    And I love you.

        Yes, my love is true,
        And I want to face
        the world with you.
        You are my fire   **t**
        All that I desire
        And I love you.

http://www.youtube.com/watch?v=9H_ZMR5IL9I
Search: # 95 if i love you ukulele man

Paintin' Them Toes

Just sittin' down here at the end of the bed
paintin' my Baby's toes.
You know how it goes paintin' them toes.
This little piggy went to market.
This little piggy stayed home
This little piggy had roast beef,
and this little piggy had none.

I repeat, my baby's feet are sweet.
I love sittin' down here at the end of the bed
paintin' my Baby's toes.
You know how it goes paintin' them toes.

Just sittin' here 'side my Baby,
given her knees a squeeze
Say "I love you , Baby" – She says "Please."
I repeat, oh my baby she's so sweet.
I love sittin' here side my Baby,
given her knees a squeeze
Say "I love you , Baby" – She says "Please."

Just lyin here side my Baby,
up close nose to nose
You know how it goes, I suppose.

This little piggy went to heaven,
after takin' off the phone
And this little piggy went
"Ooh la la" all the way home.

I repeat, my baby's feet are sweet.
I love sittin' down at the end of the bed
paintin' my Baby's toes.
Oh, you know how it goes paintin' them toes.
You know how it goes
Paintin' them toes.

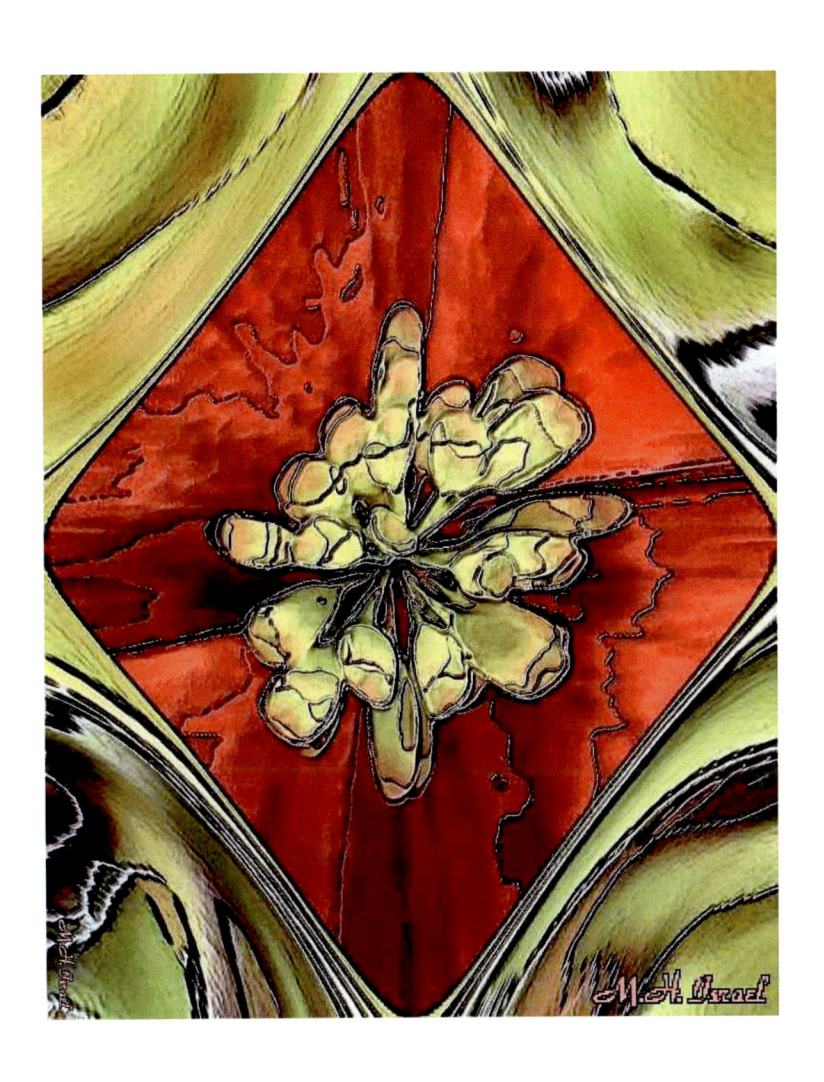

http://www.youtube.com/watch?v=30YvwcdX49o
Search: # 18 - Paintin' Them Toes (& a bit of Ted)

When I Look Into Your Eyes

When I look into your eyes
It shouldn't come as a surprise
That your beauty can hypnotize
It's true - I do love you.

When I look out at the world
I'm so happy you're my girl
Me for you and you for me
Tea for two and two for tea
It's true - I do love you.

Oh, I've been waitin'
Such a long, long time
Now, at last, you are mine
You're mine and I'm yours
And it's true - oh so true,
I do love you.

When I look out at he sun
So happy you're the one
Who cared so much about me
That you set me free
It's true - I do love you.

When I look out at the world
I'm so happy you're my girl
Me for you and you for me
Tea for two and two for tea
It's true - I do love you.
You know I do
I do love you

https://www.youtube.com/watch?v=U7l4F3hnISU
Search: #35 - Khabu & the Uke Man - When I Look Into Your Eyes

Won't you come and marry me

Won't you come and marry me
We can move out in the country
Oh how happy we will be
it's true,
Me and You

Won't you come and be my bride
stand proudly by my side
You know you are my pride
it's true,
Me and You

Won't you come and marry me
We can live in a hollow tree
Watch the butterflies fly free
it's true,
Me and You

Oh how happy we will be
it's true,
Me and You

http://www.youtube.com/watch?v=A0rSbiCbIiA
Search: # 82 Won't You Come and Marry Me

Oscar Mayer DeWine

Ohio has a Wiener
His name is Mike Dewine

He's short and bland and floppy
He doesn't have a spine

He doesn't like our questions
but he'll tell us anyway

That everything he says to us
is B-O-L-O-G-N-A

How's that?

http://www.youtube.com/watch?v=UM_VYIF48_M
Search: # 65 Ohio Has a Wiener

The Day That Superman Died

When I was just a lad,
good was good and bad was bad

'Cause Superman, by God,
was on the job

When I was just a child,
the good guys were so good
and the bad guys were so mild

'Cause Superman, by God,
was on the job

In the Land of the Free
nothin' bad could ever happen to me

'Cause Superman, by God,
was on the job

But the day
that Superman died
something died inside

Oh Lord, how we cried,
the day that Superman died.

Now Jimmy Olsen,
his favorite pal,
and Lois Lane, his number one gal

Oh, we'll all have to learn to get along some how
now that Superman has gone away.

Oh, the day that Superman died
something died inside.
Oh Lord, how we cried,

the day that Superman died.

http://www.youtube.com/watch?v=n9xy64ALPTk
Search: # 75 -- "The Day That Superman Died"

Stuporman

a son of the Greatest generation
 a father of the Alphabet
  a John the Baptist of the Big Boom
   living under the gilded "W"

Watching . . .
       . . . & Wishing:

I wish I may,
   I wish I might
      find a chunk
         of . . .
            Kryptonite

Superman has died .
and he is not the same.

Clark Kent is dead
and Bizarro Clark
stands there in his stead.

Lois is a trollop
Perry works for Fox
and Jimmy fancies signing up
to come home in a box.

And the Super one, born again,
according to god's plan,
cannot speak the language –
says, "Hi, I'm Stuporman."

Yes, he's still a man of steel,
but a smirking super fool
who would destroy the world itself
to fit it to his rule.

I wish I may,
   I wish I might
      find a chunk
         of . . .
            Kryptonite

A Package for James in England

Dear James,

    For your edification I have enclosed mementos
of our American aristocracy –
those living in the "White Castle,"
the Burghers of Columbus, so to speak.

    The contents include:
one souvenir bag embossed with Hollywood promotions;
one seductive placard singing of "The Six Pack";
AND two (2) –
        suitable as knick-knacks
        and REAL collector's items –
        cardboard White Castle hamburger containers
        (some re-assembly required).

    These latter items are ACTUAL packages
(from which the sandwiches have been removed)
and – as such –
they allow the lucky recipient
to discover the unique aroma associated with
this great American delicacy.

    If only I could send you the entire, delectable package!!

Enjoy!!

                              Yours - Tom

Too Late Smart

Can't see into the future
Can't see past my nose
Can't see into the future
Guess that's just how it goes

Too soon old
Too late smart
Old and silly
But still young at heart

      So I'll just sing a song
      An' you can feel free to sing along
      Too soon old
      Too late smart
      And no time left to start all over again

Can't see into the future
But here's some advice
Ladies and Gentlemen
pull down your pants
And slide on the ice

Can't see into the future
Can't see past my nose
But Ladies and Germs if you slide on the ice
Ya know what's gonna get froze

Won't remember the past
Can't see past my ass
Repeatin' all them mistakes
the last 'll be first and the first 'll be last

Can't see into the future
Won't remember the past
They'd put me out to pasture
But I ain't learned how to eat grass

So I'll just sing a song
An' if you feel up to it, well you can sing along
Too soon old
Too late smart
And no time left to start all over again

Too soon old
Too late smart
Old and silly
But still young at heart

Too soon old
Too late smart
Old and silly
But still young at heart

So I'll just sing a song
An' you can feel free to sing along
Too soon old
Too late smart
And no time left to start all over again

Too soon old
Too late smart
Old and silly
But still young at heart
Old and silly
But still young at heart

http://www.youtube.com/watch?v=DISHEE9EgNw
Search: Uke Man - "Too Late Smart"

Thank God for Toilets

You've got your vacuum cleaner
You've got your microwave
And you've got your lawn mower
that you borrowed from Dave,
But don't forget your toilet
'Cause when you think of it
It's the only friend you've got
That takes all your shit.

Thank God for toilets
'Cause when the shit runs down
If it weren't for toilets
We'd all be under ground.

You've got your shrinks and politicians
TV evangelists too
Oh, they listen to all your shit
But hand it back to you.
Thank God for toilets
A throne behind four walls
Where if there's ever a problem
Plumbers make house calls.

Thank God for toilets
The sewage system too
About the only thing I've got
Connecting me to all of you.
Thank God for toilets
They treat us all the same.
They take all our shit
But they don't take names.

Thank God for toilets
'Cause when the shit runs down
If it weren't for toilets
We'd all be underground.

Interred side by side, so to speak.

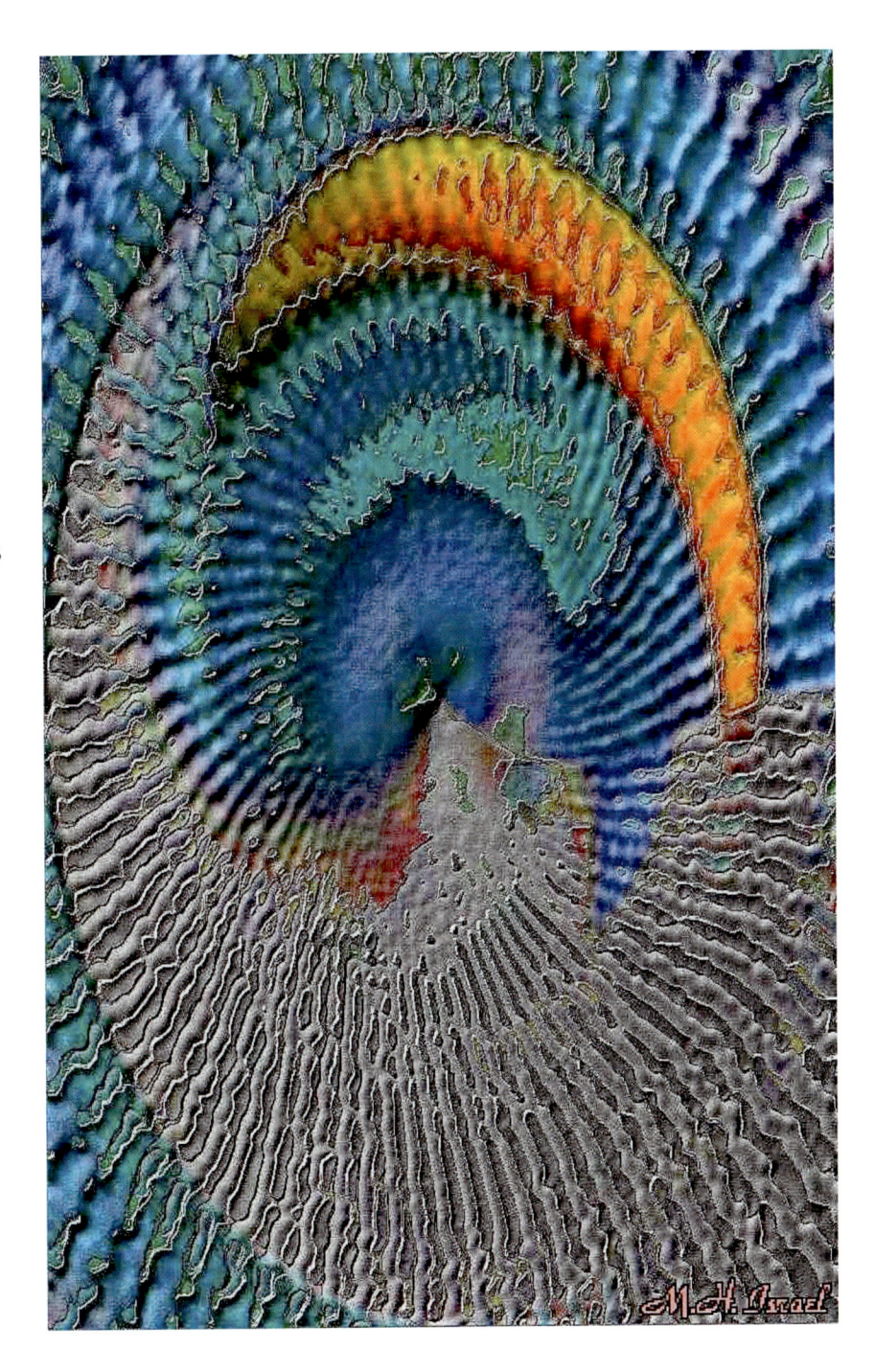

http://www.youtube.com/watch?v=xr9uzfXIv3s
Search: # 31 - Thank God for Toilets

Booger

I've got a Booger in my nose
It just sits there and grows and grows and grows

I almost choked to death last winter when it froze
Oh, I've got a Booger in my nose

Now I'm from Circleville, in the county of Pickaway
And the Boogers they grow there are the best in every way

And Booger Hospital sits at six hundred Pickaway Street
And the Boogers that they dig out there are good enough to eat

Oh, I've got a Booger in my nostril
He's a fun-lovin' Booger; he ain't hostil'

Hell, if Jesus were alive today he'd make him an apostle
I've got a Booger in my nose

Well I'm goin' down to McDonald's and without a doubt
They'll pay me for my Booger, the part what's hangin' out

They'll slice it up and fry it and put it on a bun
Oh Wendy's eat your heart out; Mickey-D's is number 1

I've got a Booger in my nose
It just sits there and grows and grows and grows

I almost choked to death last winter when it froze
Oh, I've got a Booger in my nose

Yes sir!!! Oh, I've got a Booger in my nose

https://www.youtube.com/watch?v=9vZ9mSAjNLs
Search: Uke Man Booger

Bonnie Beaver

Well, there is a homely Scottish lass
whose company I keep

And I know I'll never leave her
though to say it makes me weep

She's horsey-faced and frumpy
but I know I'll never leave her

It's not her face what keeps me here
It is her bonnie beaver

Ohhhhhhhhhhhhhhhhhhhhhhhhhhhhhh . . .

She's got an arse what's four feet wide
and lord! The girl can bitch

But when she lays back on the bed
me Johnson starts to twitch

She's a bitchy lass with a monstrous arse
but I know I'll never leave her

It's not her charms what keep me here
It is her bonnie beaver

Ohhhhhhhhhhhhhhhhhhhhhhhhhhhhhh . . .

She snorts just like an angry bull
she scratches like a cur

But, lord, somehow she knows
to make that beaver purr

She's low and mean and mangy
but I know I'll never leave her

It's not her charms what keep me here
It is her bonnie beaver

Ohhhhhhhhhhhhhhhhhhhhhhhhhhhhhh . . .

She's horsey-faced and frumpy
but I know I'll never leave her

It's not her charms what keeps me here
It is her bonnie beaver

http://www.youtube.com/watch?v=RMQjrIQz5I4   Search: # 86 Bonny Beaver

Niagara Viagra

(spoken introduction)

*Poor old Bob Dole lost the election
and things looked pretty bad,
but he lucked out
Got himself a job sellin' drugs
for a large pharmaceutical corporation
and the money just kept pourin' in
since there wasn't any stiff competition
so to speak.
Bob thought he and Liddy
could live there forever
in the Watergate Apartments
in Washington the town he loved so much.
But just leave it to a guy like Bill Clinton
to screw something up.
Yeah, along came that scandal and cast a pall over
Washington.
It really bothered Bob, sorta ate at him
until one day he couldn't stand it any more
and he took Liddy by the hand and he said,
"Come on, Girl, were gonna go for a walk."
And he took her out into the late afternoon
and started makin' their way to the Mall, and
in time, as the stars were just starting
to push through the darkening sky
Bob led Liddy up the many steps of the Capitol
way up high, next to the dome.
He turned her around and looked down the Mall
at that great Freudian erection to the memory
of the Father of our Country, the Washington Monument,
the stiffest thing in Washington outside of Al Gore.
And with the monument reflecting in Liddy's eyes
Bob embraced her and tenderly he said:*

"Let's take a trip with Viagra
I'll have you climbin' the walls
chemical passion is really in fashion
let's get away from the Mall.

We can forget about Clinton
forget about Monica too.
We'll go to Niagara; I'll take Viagra

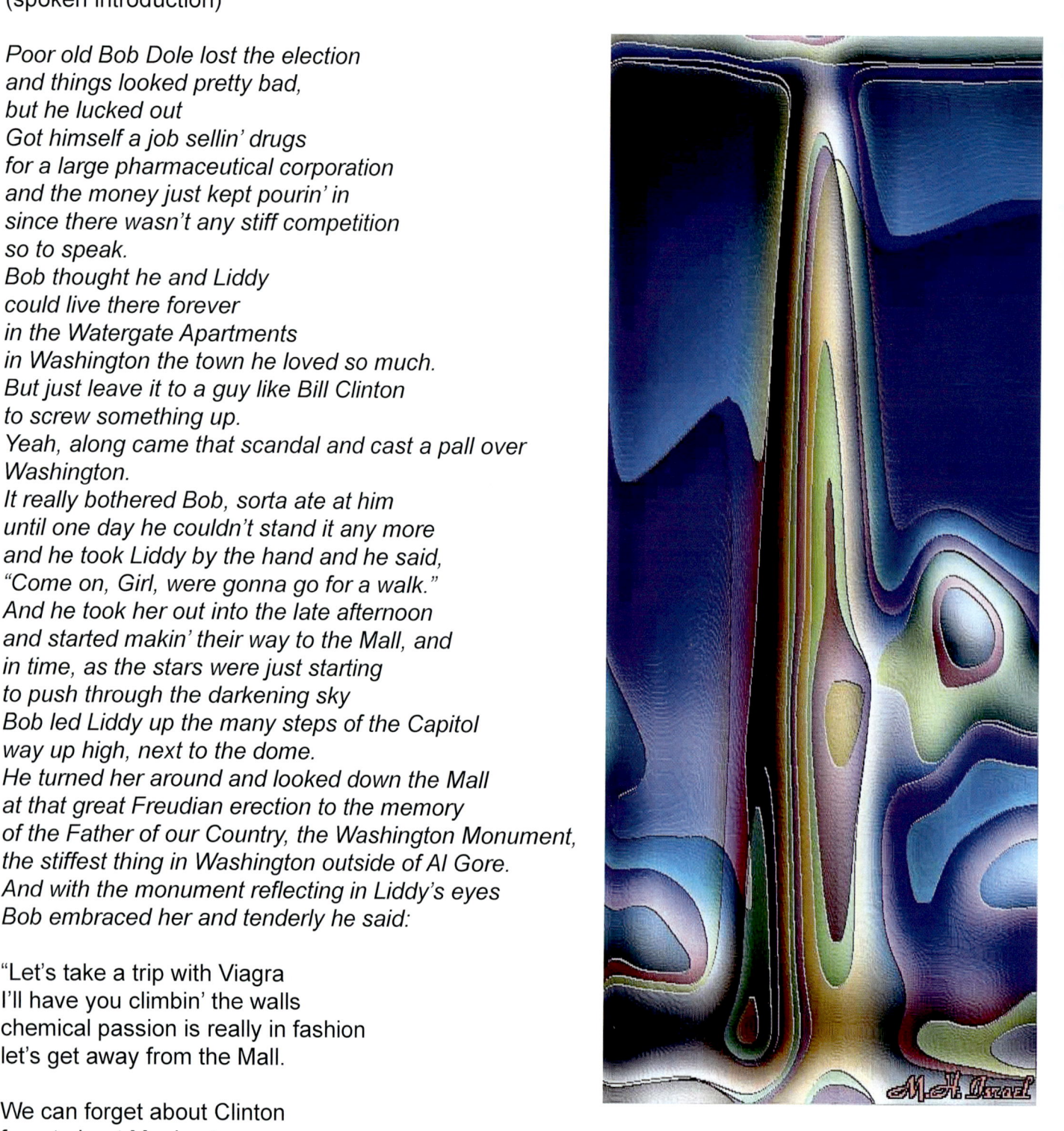

and we'll do what the Democrats do.
You can buy a new outfit,
throw in a black negligee.
Oh, we'll go to Niagara; I'll take Viagra
and you better stand back out of the way.

We can forget about Clinton
forget old Henry Hyde too
Oh, we'll go to Niagara; I'll take Viagra
the rest of it Babe's up to you.

I'm tellin' you, Doll, my boy will stand tall
Let's get away from the Mall

 I've got some samples

Let's get away from the Mall."

http://www.youtube.com/watch?v=jcKrFotDoUA
Search: # 105 - Niagara Viagra

I'm Tired of God (short version)

I'm tired of God.
I've had enough of Him!
Him & his crap!

Yeah! He beat me when I was little
when I didn't know shit!
Yeah! and He strutted around
all holier than thou
(as if He really *knew* thou) !

Well, that was then !
I never see him now !

Holy Roller Polka

Well, you can't be a Holy Roller if you're rollin' in the hay
Gotta thump upon your Bible, gotta thump it every day
You can't be a Holy Roller, 'less you walk the narrow way
You can't be a Holy Roller if you're rollin' in the hay

But you can be a Holy Roller and vote for David Duke
You can be a Holy Roller and be a wild-eyed kook
You can be a Holy Roller if Limbaugh is your man
You can be a Holy Roller and a wizard in the Ku Klux Klan

But you can't be a Holy Roller if you drink or smoke or chew
You can't be a Holy Roller if you like to play cards or screw.

But you can be a Holy Roller – do what the TV evangelists do
You can drink & smoke & chew & screw if nobody's watching you

So, I'm gonna be a Holy Roller. I know it will be hard.
I'm gonna be a Holy Roller and get myself straight with God
I'm gonna be a Holy Roller;
 I really hope I can
'Cause I wanna be a Holy Roller and a wizard in the Ku Klux Klan
I wanna be a Holy Roller and a wizard in the Ku Klux Klan.

Oh, do the Holy Roller Polka as you dance around the floor
Find someone to kick and give 'em "what for"
Find someone to blame your sins on then kick 'em some more
Do the Holy Roller Polka and march right out the door
There ain't nobody keepin' score

Do the Holy Roller Polka.

http://www.youtube.com/watch?v=-O4fOk-xWdk
Search: Ty & the Uke Man - "Holy Roller Polka"

Askin' Questions

I'm just sittin' and thinkin' and wonderin' and askin' questions
'bout why it has to be this way
And I don't really know what it is I'm supposed to do
Or what I'm supposed to say

And I could sit and think and wonder here forever
And I still wouldn't know what it is I'm supposed to do
Or what I'm supposed to say

And I really wish it could be different
And I wish it could turn out some other way
But I could sit and think and wonder here forever
And Kafka and I would still be stuck inside this demented play

Do you think there'll be a surprise ending?
Deus ex Machina for me
Do you think there'll be a surprise ending?
When at last I am set free . . .

Yeah, I could sit and think and wonder here forever
And I still wouldn't know what it is I'm supposed to do
Or what I'm supposed to say

But when I'm in your arms, I don't ask questions
And I always seem to find the things I need to say
And at the end of every day when I'm lost, sad, and blue
At the end of every day the road leads back to you

Do you think we'll have a happy ending?
Do you think we'll get out of here alive?
We could sit and wait here for Godot
But , then, I've heard he won't arrive

I'm just sittin' and thinkin' and wonderin' and askin' questions
'bout why it has to be this way
And I still don't really know what it is I'm supposed to do
Or what I'm supposed to say

And I could sit and think and wonder here forever, 'til my dyin' day
But when it's over and done and through
I know what I will do
I'll just stop and think of you

And float away

http://www.youtube.com/watch?v=uThuGrVP6dY
Search: # 84 Asking Questions

When I Unwrap the Fruitcake

When I unwrap the fruitcake
from its silver shroud,
layer upon layer
of ever more convoluted, evolved, and faceted
foil,
I almost shrink from the sight of the inner
more sacred shroud
(Turin is discredited – but not this)

the cloth with its inter-weavings strikes my mind,
a net to hold, a skin to preserve, and
each time
it must be stripped
to leave the naked delasciviousness of itself
each time it must lie bare before me to feel the pleasure
of my knife

it came from love, from god
for he so loved the world that he
breathed life into plants and beasts and men
and women

and they saw that it was good and bore fruit and the fruit was good
and worthy
and the woman took of the fruit and manipulated it as if she were
a god unto herself (for the serpent had beguiled her)

and she gave it to the man as an offering and he unwrapped her

tenderly he unwrapped her
tenderly he placed his edge against her
tenderly he split her
and made her whole.

When I unwrap the fruitcake from its shroud
new life stirs in me
stirred from the fruit of love's labor past
not lost
that touches my eye
my nose
my tongue

and my serpent.

Pinocchio Knows

Geppetto was a lonely man
he carved a boy from wood
He wasn't much at anatomy
but he whittled pretty good

He left the boy without some parts
but he gave him a wondrous nose
When stimulated properly
it grows and grows and grows

Well, he's a big hit with the women
They're all in love with him
and if he noses 'bout their business
it doesn't bother them

In fact when lifting up their skirts
to show their tender thighs
they hold the boy by both his ears
and insist that he tell lies

Jiminy Cricket was his friend
his conscience, don't ya know
but Jiminy was a voyeur
He loved to watch the show

He never ever tugged his arm
He never would intrude
to warn against his manly charm
to say his nose was lewd

Well, he's all the rage in Italy
in Europe and beyond
His paramours all love his nose
They call the boy Don Wand

And husbands know to keep close guard
'cause a nose of wood is always hard
They curse and moan and wish him dead
this low-down wooden head

Still, Fortune smiled on Pinocchio
until one fateful winter
when his haughty lover the Queen of Spain
took a nasty splinter

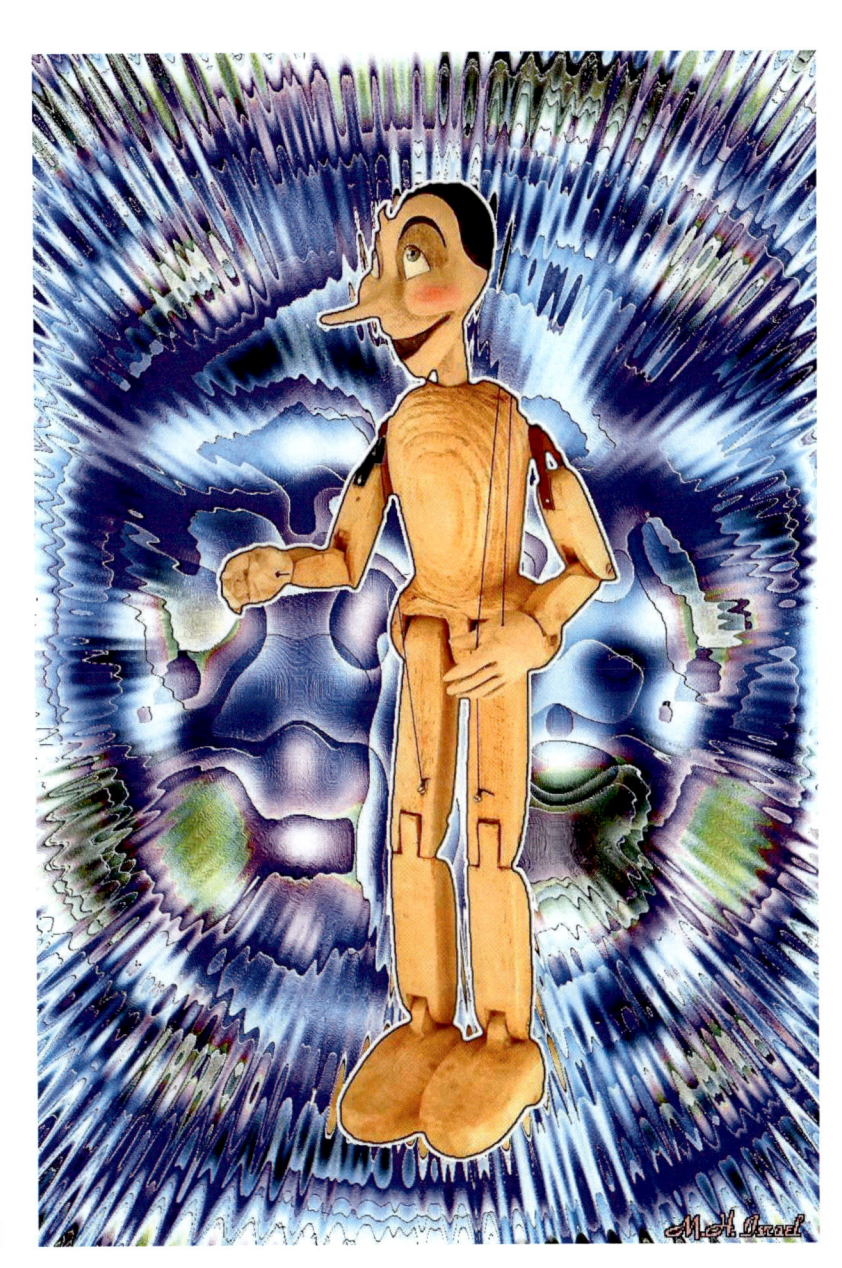

The Executioner accosted him
but Pinocchio slipped away
and I hear he's alive and well
and livin' in the USA

Those few American girls who've found him
all say the boy's a prize
They love to sit for hours
and listen to his lies

So if you come across him
hangin' out at the Mall
don't miss your chance to try him on
One size fits all

He's a real live boy
and that's the truth

        http://www.youtube.com/watch?v=GahtxCyN-10   Search: # 94 Pinocchio Knows

These Guts

I carry these guts 'round inside me
an' I know that they're not
what they were.

I'm told it's the lifestyle
I'm living.

I'm rotten.
I need to be pure.

But the good are dying around me.
Their jogging, their diet's
no cure.

The good are dying around me.
So,
Shithead,

don't feel so secure.

Crazy Over You

I'm tired of being alone
Won't you call me on the phone
Just call me up and say, "Hi!"

I really love you, Baby, yes I do
There's nobody else for me but you!

Come on and give a ring
That'd be such a sweet thing
To call and tell me I'm your guy.

I really love you, Baby;
and you know I don't mean maybe
I can't think of anything but you,

And when I hear your voice,
I have no choice.
I'm so crazy over you.

Come on and give a ring
Come on and be a sweet thing
Come on and tell me I'm your guy.

Come on and give a ring
Come on tell me I'm your sweet thing
If I don't hear your voice I'll die.

And when I hear your voice,
I have no choice.
I just fall more in love with you.

I'm so crazy over you.

http://www.youtube.com/watch?v=dFZe1V2TLXk
Search: # 88 Crazy Over You

Spam-Eatin' Blues

I ain't nothin' but a hound dog
I'm a poor excuse for a man

Since you left me Baby
all I've got left's this here can of Spam

> Oh, I don't know what I'm gonna do
> Yeah, I've got this here can of Spam
> but Baby I ain't got you

Breakfast, lunch, and dinner
it's all the same damned thing
Processed pork can get me by
but it can't make me sing

> Oh, I've got the Spam-eatin blues
> And I think I would rather be
> eatin' one of your shoes

Oh, come home cookin' Mama
and bring your juicy ham
Bring them luscious loaves of bread
come home and feed your man

> Oh, I don't know what I'm gonna do
> Yeah, I've got this here can of Spam
> but Baby I ain't got you

Still got some pickle relish
Savin' it just for you
Oh come home cookin' Mama
and see what we can do

> Oh, I don't know how I'm gonna get on
> Yeah, I've got this here can of Spam
> but there ain't no Gray Poupon

> No Gray Poupon !

> http://www.youtube.com/watch?v=2MVSukb7M0k
> Search: Spam Blues at Fat's

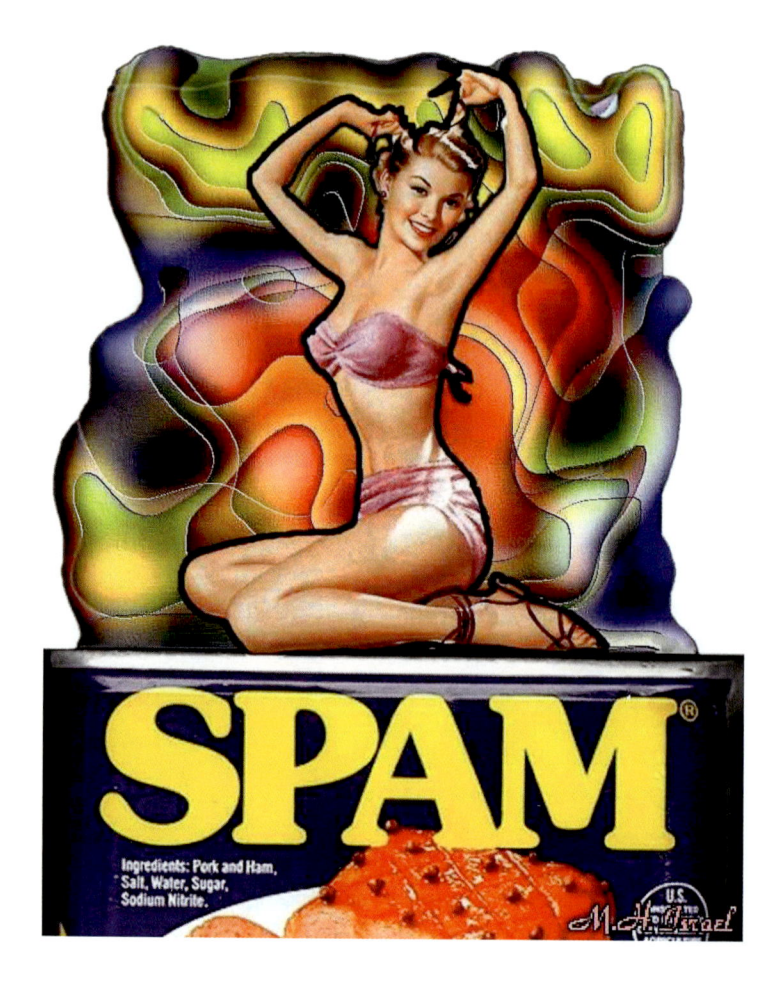

Monster In the White House

There's a Monster in the White House
There's a Monster in DC
There's a Monster in the White House
With his eye on you and me.

    And he's never known a pain
    And he's always had his way
    And he always will
        Unless we stand up some day

His thugs are in the Statehouse
And in the Courthouse too
And his Trolls are in our cities
Watching what we do

And they all bow down to Mammon
And worship gold and green
While greasing up the levers
Of their grizzly death machine

There's a ghoul inside the presses
And a third eye in the flag
And the lady of the harbor
Is a bent and twisted hag

There's a vampire in the blood-bank
And a zombie on TV
And a vulture on the lamp post
Making plans for you and me

And they've never known a pain
And they've always had their way
And they always will
'Til we stand up some day

There's a gargoyle in the bedroom
Elmer Gantry's in the schools
And the monster in the Whitehouse
Just smirks and struts and drools

But he was never called a faggot
never called a dirty Jew, and
he never heard Louis Armstrong
singin' "Black & Blue"

And he's never known a pain
And he's always had his way
And he always will
Unless we stand up someday

So let's all get up-stand up together now
Let's all get up-stand up together now
Let's all get up-stand up together now
And make the monster pay

http://www.youtube.com/watch?v=WhDr7SHVDn4
Search: Ty & the Uke Man - "Monster in the White House"

Dick Army

There's a Dick Armey down in Texas;
there's a Dick Armey in D.C.

There's a Dick Armey all over this land
trying to stick it to you and me.

And he likes to wrap up in the flag,
and he don't like "Barney Fag,"

and he says Hillary is a hag,
Oh, Dickie, you're such a drag.

But, Dickie, you ain't got the only Army –
No - We've got a Dick Army too.

So, get ready to dance
When we unzip our pants

We're gonna piss all over you
with our Dick Army.

We're gonna piss all over you;
Ready, Aim, Fire !!

We're gonna piss all over you !

http://www.youtube.com/watch?v=ctHL0hfWroU
Search: # 48 - Battle Hymn of the Dick Army

The Giants and Worms Among Men

The Giants are great and slovenly and walk upon us, but they are the Giants, and it doesn't matter to them that they squash us. At most, our bones provide but small shock to the calloused gravity of their feet.

It is nothing to them. They are the Giants, oblivious, and even if (somehow) they could be shaken into consciousness, the Worms that whisper in their ears would eat their nascent thoughts and pass them on as wormy excrement.

We adapt, do the best we can, curse the Giants, curse the Worms, curse one another, curse our own "worms" for cursing us for *our* cursing. But nothing changes. We are the victims of the Giants and the Worms, and have been - ever since the first words of man were scratched on rocks. There was a time, some say, before the Giants and the Worms . . . when we were free.

I would like to be free . . . I think. But it is difficult to imagine life without our masters. And, it is possible that things were not so good even *before* the Giants.

Whatever it was like, we are not supposed to speak of it or even think of it.

Still, many of us do, and that is why our own little, self-important man-worms rail at us, demanding that the ancient laws be followed - to appease the gods, to keep us safe, to maintain what they call our *prosperity*.

They preach new laws too, derived (they say) from the old laws, but it is a strange prosperity that we enjoy under all these Holy laws.

It is said that we - here - who "respect the law and honor our betters" - are particularly fortunate and are less frequently trod upon by the Great Ones (men in other lands, we know for a certainty, are *eaten* by their Giants).

Old Marbo claims that she has seen *our* Giants eating people too, but it *is* possible they were only evildoers brought here from another land.

I do not know.

   * * *

"Work saves us," says Da'miller, our man-worm overseer. If that is true, then why do I not know it? I have known enough of work to have been saved long ago.

" Work is salvation." What Wormshit!!

   * * *

There is something wrong with these men, these worms who would be Worms. *They* can never be Worms; they can only be pale, slimy imitations of the great, ugly beasts who whisper in the Giants' ears. Yet *they* slobber and bow in the presence of an actual Worm, transported by the orgasmic desire to kiss and lick its body, to eat its excrement, digest it, and produce it anew for us to wallow in as if it were their own.

Oh yes, we men wallow in it, to be sure. Many of us even take pride in it, and those who don't are guaranteed to feel the wrath of those who do. These would-be Worms stand there, dripping shit and marketing their odor as an aphrodisiac, denigrating all who are not stained with subservience.

Oh supreme irony! *They* - basking in their Holiness - are the supreme sinners of mankind, the craven cowards who are not content with ending *their* human lives, but must end *ours* as well. Worms within worms within worms within worms - eating their putrid selves and demanding that we praise them for it - demanding that we emulate their ecstatic living death and so assuage the terrible guilt they feel but cannot face.

So be it. Let them eat themselves. Let them eat their masters' shit and smear it upon themselves as a badge of honor. Let them parade before us smirking with pride in their utter degradation.

   . . . but I will not be moved.

Clothes Make the Man #1

     Clothes make the man

     So, when I die
     Bury my clothes

     When I murder
     Arrest my clothes

     Execute them
         Or
     (if the Republicans are out)
     Give them life imprisonment without chance of parole

     Make love to my clothes
     take them off caressingly
     and take the money from the pockets
     (they won't notice)

     Impregnate my clothes
     and bring forth progeny
     of patches and rags

     a gauche immortality

     spawn of moths' balls

I Like Your Haircut

I like your haircut; I like your haircut.
I like the way it sits up on your head.

I like your haircut; I like your haircut.
I bet it looks like that when you get out o' bed!

    Well, did you do it yourself,
    Or did your wife lend you a hand?
    Oh, Eddie, with that haircut you're one hell of a man!

I like your haircut; I like your haircut.
I like the way it drapes down 'round your skull.
I like your haircut; I like your haircut.
Did you get it done here in town or up at the mall?

    Well, it wasn't at J's, but somewhere where it pays
    To be seen by the cultural elite
    And it pays in many ways, like windy days
    When your head looks like a fresh-plucked sugar beet.

I like your haircut; I like your haircut.
I like the way it sprouts from your cranium.
I like your haircut; I like your haircut;
Reminds me of my Granny's geranium.

Well, does it impress the girls
What you've done to your curls?
Do the union folks at the plant all kiss your feet?
Does your secretary swoon when you walk into the room
And that bird's nest on your head begins to tweet?

Oh, I like your haircut; I like your haircut.
I bet it looks like that when you get out o' bed!

http://www.youtube.com/watch?v=OBmo8CJY_T0
Search: # 53 - "I Like Your Haircut" - Ty & the Uke Man

Clothes Make the Man #2

Then god said,   "Let us make man in our own image,"

And He formed man of
35% cotton and 65% polyester
and
breathless -
like Jerry Lee -
gave man Great Balls
of Fire

(god also made woman –
from one of man's collar stays –
but that is another story)

    So

Remember man that thou art cloth,

food for hungry
moths

moths which
once
(when they were worms)
ate up
the meaty men
of yore

but now must try to
earn their wings
digesting polyester things,
and gumming wool and cotton strings,

to eat the Men of Cloth.

Eldorado

I'm just drivin' all around in my 1984 beat-up Cadillac
It's almost as beat up as me
I'm just drivin' all around town in my old Cadillac
Headin' for Eldorado and I ain't comin' back

    Just drivin' all around in my Caddy
    My cat, myself and I, and Daddy
    Just drivin' all around in my car
    Gonna win the lottery, gonna be a star

Oh, have you seen the hills that they must climb
In the Olympic Marathon
Well, I couldn't even walk up one of them
But I ain't gonna have no hills to climb
When I finally arrive, when I finally arrive in New York City

    Just drivin' all around in New York City
    Dad, myself and I, and kitty
    Through the Mountains of the Moon and the Valley of the Shadow
    Just makin' my way to Eldorado

Oh, have you seen the hills that folks must climb
Who live in New York City
Well, I couldn't even crawl up one of them
But I ain't gonna have no hills to climb
When I finally arrive, when I finally arrive in New York City

    Just drivin' all around in New York City
    Dad, myself and I, and kitty
    Just drivin' all around in my auto
    Through the Mountains of the Moon and the Valley of the Shadow
    Just makin' my way to Eldorado
    Gonna be a star
    Gonna win the Lotto

    http://www.youtube.com/watch?v=CbvdqPypc5g
    Search: # 15 - Eldorado Tom Harker

Maybe I'll

Sittin' here watchin' the walls all alone
Three or four hours 'til my Baby gets home
Wish there was somethin' I could do
Help me out, Folks, I don't have a clue

Well, maybe I could get my belly button pierced
Maybe I could buy-me a Sega CD-Player
Maybe buy some o' that spray-on hair
Spray me on another layer

Maybe I could get me a big ol' tattoo
Sounds like somethin' that I might do
Or maybe just take a walk out to the zoo
Sounds good to me, does it sound good to you?

Or maybe I could buy me a new pair o' shoes
Stop at the store and get me some booze
Drink it all down as I walk around town
Sounds good to me, I got nothin' to lose

Maybe I should buy me some hashish or pot
Get me a date with old Margie Schott
Sit around, commiserate about Pete Rose
And knock off her socks with my Schwarzenegger pose

Or maybe I should go down to Disney World
And see if I can find me that Kerrigan girl
Get a Lille hammer and bang on her knee
Sound good to you? Well, it sounds good to me

Or maybe I could buy a Fishin' Pocket Popeil
Or get me a suit and act like a wheel
Call up the Donald and write up a deal
Then look up Madonna and cop me a feel

But all of my maybe's they cost lots of money
Maybe I should just go lay out someplace sunny
And work a couple hours on my charms
So I can roll around in my sweet Baby's arms

Rollin' all around in my sweet Baby's arms
Rollin' all around in my sweet Baby's charms
Buy me some crackers from Pepperidge Farms
And roll in the crumbs in my sweet baby's arms

Rollin' all around in my sweet Baby's arms
Rollin' all around listening to her purr

Meowwwwwwwwwwwwww

Sounds good to me,
Hope it sounds good to her.

                              https://www.youtube.com/watch?v=v2P-76vtEMg
                              Search: # 60 - "Maybe I'll" Ty & the Uke Man

What a Strange Thing

Oh what a strange thing
to be a bird and not take wing.

"To dream a dream
of soaring high
while sitting here until I die,
singing a song of right and wrong
and doing both
though
I don't know why,
as sun & moon go whirling by,"

is a wrong song to sing.

Gold is gold
and old is old,
and the first and last are for the bold.

Whether heat of day or cool of night,
(whether all is wrong or all is right)
take wing and sing;
don't sit and die.

There's time for sitting,
bye and bye

when there's only one.

Daddy & Aaron Went Camping

When Daddy and Aaron went camping
They had a mighty good time
Woke up so early in the morning
To see the sun rise and shine

And Aaron found a lucky feather
And he put it in his hat
Yes he found a lucky feather
Hey boys, what do you think of that !!

https://www.youtube.com/watch?v=03padwQR8zo
Search: # 90 - "When Daddy & Aaron Went Camping" - October 8, 2009

Sittin' Down at Shifty's

I'm just sittin' down at Sifty's spendin' all my dough
What little bit I got, easy come easy go
So, Honey, if you please, come give a squeeze
And buy me a couple more beers

Kenny and Sparky come in every day
And every now and then, I see my old friend Ray
They all sit down beside me and slap me on the back
And buy me a couple more beers

I'm just an old worn-out country boy doin' the best I can
Tryin' to convince myself that I am still a man
So, Honey, if you please, come give a squeeze
And buy me a couple more beers

My mind goes back to Grandpa's place where I had some fun
Grandma & Grandpa said I was their favorite one
But that was long ago and so far away
Now I sit in Shifty's everyday

I'm just an old worn-out country boy sittin' on my stool,
Tryin' to convince myself that I am not a fool.
I've got no place to go and nothin' much to do
And every now and then I think of you

Oh, I open up ol' Shifty's everyday at 8:00
I'm always on time; I ain't hardly ever late
Mona lets me in, sets me up a double gin
And buys me a couple more beers

I'm just an old worn-out country boy doin' the best I can
Tryin' to convince myself that I am still a man
So, Honey, if you please, come give a squeeze
And buy me a couple more beers
Ohhh , Honey, if you please
come give a squeeze

And buy me . . . a couple more beers

        http://www.youtube.com/watch?v=MVG1xxw8dOk
        Search: "Sittin' Down at Shifty's" Redux

Tiny Oaks

  Tiny oaks
  From mighty acorns growing.

  The harvest is less
  Than the sowing.

Redwood Tree

I went to California to look at the trees
And there they were, as big as you please.
Holdin' up the sky and stuck in God's eye
Unmoved by the breeze.

Old enough to 've been in Jesus' cross,
as old as when Julie Caesar was boss,
And if you count the stumps in the park,
As old as the wood in Noah's Ark.

Oh, I think that I shall never see
More clearly immortality
than that view given to me
When I saw the redwood tree

Two thousand years, at least, I'm told,
Before a redwood is considered old
But it seems it could be more:
If two thousand, why not four?

But as of now when they fall down,
They're just left there lying on the ground
'Til lumbermen practice their subtle arts
and haul away the Redbeard's parts.

But if a tree falls down and can't get up,
Why not before we sleep or sup
Bring in pulleys, cables and a crane;
set that sucker up again

Tamp its roots into the ground,
fertilize and water all around,
And promise to the Redwood glade
eternal Redwood Medicaid.

And though we cannot make
our sun stand still,
yet we can make it run.

Oh . . . I went to California to look at the trees
and there they were, as big as you please.
Holdin' up the sky and stuck in God's eye
Made quite an impression on me.
Me and the tree and immortality.

http://www.youtube.com/watch?v=5kjTToXK1Kl
Search: # 59 - Redwood Tree

Cornucopia

C is for the Cornucopia of blandness
H is for the Happy Days that seldom come
A is for the Appetites that hold us near
O is for "Oh my god, My dear."
S is for the silly song I'm singing - - -
put them all together they spell LOVE

    put it in a box and throw away the key
    don't let Pandora near
    put it in a box and throw away the key
    then go and have another beer

C is for the cornucopia of meanness
H is for the Holiness that never shows
A is for the Afterlife that keeps us in line
O is for "Oh my god, there's nothing there."
S is for the silly song I'm singing - - -
put them all together they spell LIFE

    put it in a box and throw away the key
    don't let Pandora near
    put it in a box and throw away the key
    then go and have another beer

C is for the cornucopia of self-deception
H is for the Holy Wars we wage
A is for the Asylum that we live in
O is for "Oh no, we'll never change!!
S is for the silly song I'm singing - - -
put them all together they spell MAN.

    put it in a box and throw away the key
    don't let Pandora near
    put it in a box and throw away the key
    then go and have another beer

C is for the cornucopia of Bullying
H is for the Hydrogen Bomb
A is for the Animals in charge of us
O is for "Oh damn, now it's done."
S is for the silly song I'm singing - - -
put them all together they spell DOOM

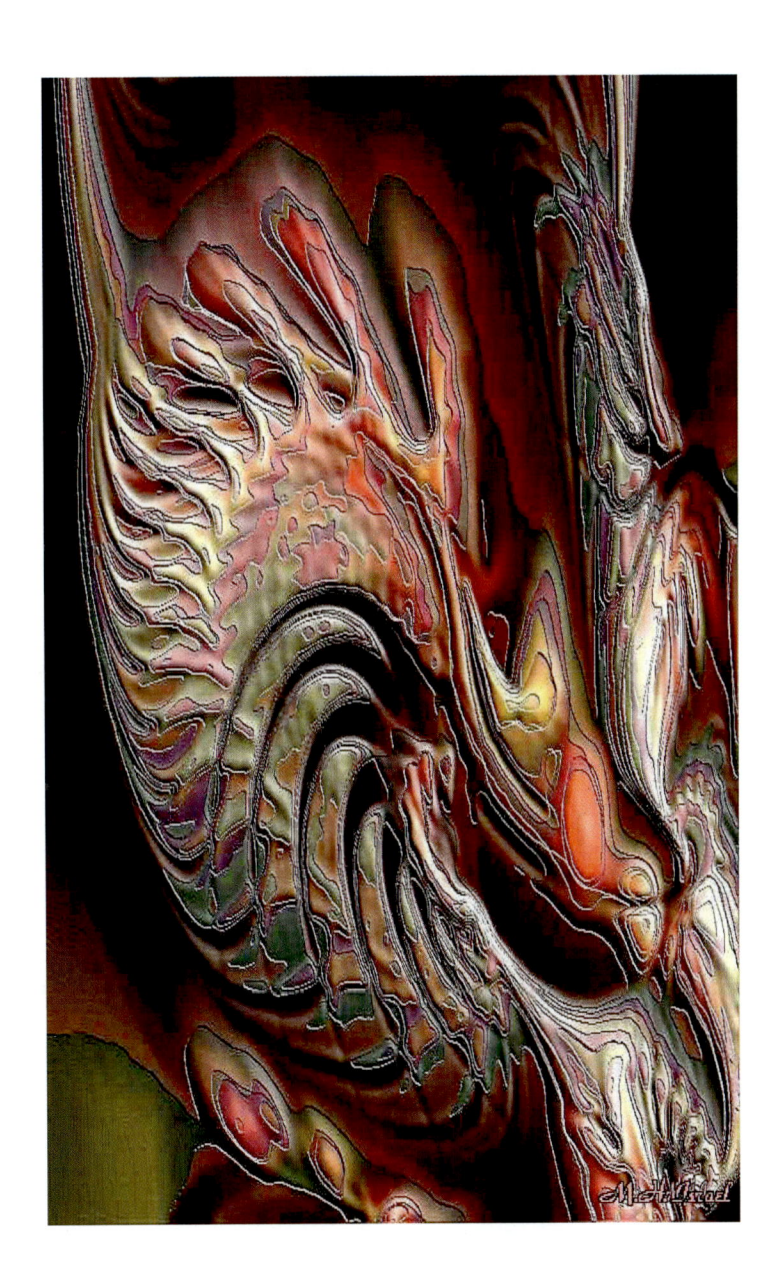

Put it in a box and throw away the key
Don't let Pandora near
Put it in a box and throw away the key
Then go and have another beer
Then go and have another beer
Then go and have another beer
Then go and have another beer

https://www.youtube.com/watch?v=E39tw9eKO_k
Search: Ukulele Man - "Cornucopia"

I Had a Dream Last Night

I had a dream last night
What a lovely dream it was
I had a dream last night
Livin' in the land of Oz

Everybody was so happy
Everybody was so gay
I had a dream last night
But I woke up today

Everybody was talkin' at me
Tellin' me what to do
But then I woke up and they were gone

Even you

I'm just lookin' in the mirror
And what do I see?
Just a sad reflection
Lookin' back at me

And Morning always seems to follow night
And everything that was so right
Disappears with the first light
Of day

I had a dream last night
What a lovely dream it was
I had a dream last night
Livin' in the land of Oz

Everybody was so happy
Everybody was so gay
I had a dream last night
But I woke up today

http://www.youtube.com/watch?v=IdKHZmj2AaY
Search: # 63 - "I Had a Dream Last Night

Left Behind

Waiting for the Rapture, reading Revelations, waiting to be "Left Behind" - earnestly anticipating Ned Flanders' disappearance – mid frame – along with all his annoying pals. Leaving their clothes and glasses and watches behind to float for an instant in the empty air – ball caps and bifocals; Rolexes and pacemakers; colostomy bags and surprised toupees mourning their absent pates; pairs of silicon balloons undulating pointlessly, vacant wooden legs standing at attention, and glass eyes (round like marbles) – floating as if painted by Dali - floating - floating - floating for an endless instant – until Newton notices and ends the unnatural levitation – the incongruous delegates falling *at last* - only to reconvene in piles upon their 7,000 year old, fossil encrusted mother. Pulled there – this unexpected collection of inorganic human parts – by the predestined parlor trick
of an Almighty god !!!

All the bright-eyed, smiling, fetus-waving, homo-hating, self-righteous, patriarchal zombies vaporized into the clouds to join Jim Jones in holy oblivion or to wear their Nikes on Haley-Bop's backside. They should be happy! They loved to harp on earth – they can harp forever there – and wear white past Labor Day! - Hosanna !!! Hosanna !!! On high !!

Epilogue –

Flanders is gone, and all his crew -
Left us behind . . .

gone to Heaven
and can't come back –

left us alone . . .
at last

and though Hell be warm, it's safe
(there are no *good* folks there).

I Love You and You Love Me

I love you and you love me
And baby that's how it's always gonna be
Lovin' you and lovin' me

I don't know, but I've been told
The streets of heaven are paved with gold
And hearts and souls are bought and sold

It's true, oh yes, I know – I know, do you?

But you kiss me and I'll kiss you
And, Baby, that's gonna pull us through
Kissin' me and kissin' you

I don't know, but I've been told
The Devil's kisses are mighty cold
And hearts and souls are bought and sold

It's true, oh yes, I know – I know, do you?

So, you touch me and I'll touch you
And, Baby, that's gonna pull us through
Touchin' me and touchin' you

I don't know but I guess it's true
Better stay here on earth with you
And our love will pull us through

It's true, oh yes, I know – I know, do you?

You love me and I'll love you
And Baby that's gonna pull us through
Lovin' me and Lovin' you

It's true

http://www.youtube.com/watch?v=89gGPExtZ1U&feature=youtu.be
Search: # 111 - I Love You and You Love Me

Jesus Chrysler

I got in my old LeBaron, and I drove to the sacred store,
and a fellah said, "Can I help you, brother?" as I walked in through the door.
I said, "I think you can, my man, 'cause I've got a simple wish.
I want a chrome or plastic stick-on Jesus fish."

Well, the deal went down without a hitch, and I didn't have to pay no tax.
I slapped that baby on the back o' my LeBaron and sat down to relax.
I found the ignition, yeah and I turned the key,
gonna drive that Jesus Chrysler from here to eternity.

When you're drivin' a Jesus Chrysler, everyone makes way for you;
even at the Pearly Gates they just smile and wave you through,
and there is Michael the Archangel with a bucket in his hand
just waitin' to wash your car as it enters the Promised Land.

Well, I'm winnin' all my football bets with Jesus on my team
and the lord's lookin' over my liver - it's me, the lord, and Jim Beam.
The landlord he's forgot my name; he doesn't bother me,
and the US postal service sends my letters out for free.

I'm winnin' on the slots over at the casino, and all of my bets out at the track
are win, place, and show. All my friends at the 7- Eleven
say I'll win the lottery. And nobody cares if I show up for work;
they just mail the check to me.

When you're drivin' a Jesus Chrysler, you're bound to go far,
and it don't really take too much, just a fish stuck on your car.
When you're drivin' a Jesus Chrysler, that's a sacred car;
you've got the right credentials; you're a Jesus Chrysler super star.

I'm appearin' on the 700 Club; Pat Robertson's in love with me,
and I find myself at the top of the charts with my Christian rap CD.
All my Jewish friends have converted; my gay friends have gone straight too,
and I've even got the monkeys testifyin' to their trainers out at the zoo.

Since I've advertised for Jesus, he's been takin' care of me.
Now I can get my cable, and I don't have to pay no fee.
Yeah, I can walk on water (if the water ain't too deep),
and I even told the IRS to take a flyin' leap.

http://www.youtube.com/watch?v=CDPF7G7Gn6s
Search: Ukulele Man & his Prodigal Sons - "Jesus Chrysler"

So if success and salvation are what you truly wish,
get a Chrysler, Dodge, or Plymouth and stick on a Jesus fish.
Oh you'll be drivin' a Jesus Chrysler, that's a sacred car.
And you're guaranteed a place in heaven. You're a Jesus Chrysler super star.
Oh yeah, You're guaranteed a place in heaven. You're a Jesus Chrysler super star.

Sacramental Wine

Father Culliton took a swig of sacramental wine
Said, "Don'tcha worry Billy-boy, it's but a habit of mine
You know I'm old and I like to think about the blessed ending time
When we'll all be with Jesus and we'll all be doin' fine"

Well, the altar boy took a swig himself – it was his habit, too
And he placed the bottle back upon the shelf as he was wont to do
And both the lads were feelin' fine and thus fortified at last
They burst into the church to say the mornin' mass

Well, they made it through the Introit, Latin flyin' at full tilt
Yeah, they said it then in Latin, but with an Irish lilt
'Twas near the Offertory when with a slurping sound
The old man's ill-fit dentures fell out upon the ground

Well, the mass went on – as it should – and never missed a beat
Save for one strange English phrase, "Bill, pick up me goddamned teeth"
And they both thought of Jesus and the blessed ending time
And they knew that this, too, would pass
And they'd be doin' fine

So, let's all take a swig for ourselves and drink to the priest and Bill
And have another round and try to get our fill
But let's not think of Jesus and the blessed ending time
Just have another swig of sacramental wine

And pass around the bottle one more time

http://www.youtube.com/watch?v=HlH0pni5U2w
Search: # 8 - Sacramental Wine

Diffusion

My mother,
fragile, translucent,
bent,
as if hovering over the world
to make all things right
with her gentle
hands

Whether I live or die
doesn't matter,
but I fear
her death.

Goin' to the Grocery with My Mom

Goin' to the grocery with my Mom
I'm sittin' in the cart - we roll a long
I create the chatter Momma hums a song
Goin' to the grocery with my Mom

She puts Bisquick & Ovaltine sauerkraut and navy beans
Wonder bread and butter in the cart
Maxwell House and coffee cake, Crisco and Frosted Flakes
And the little boy she loves with all her heart

Goin' to the grocery with my Mom
Sittin' in the cart we roll along
I provide the chatter
Momma hums a song
Goin' to the grocery with my Mom

But the road leads on
And the sea rolls in
And things do change
Once they begin

And the road leads on –
That's life's plan
And a little boy
Grows up to be a man –
Goin' to the grocery with his Mom

Goin' to the grocery with my Mom
She leans on the cart - I tag along
We get liverwurst and rye bread
Sweet-dills from up high
And a can of pumpkin for a pie

We put crackers and pimento cheese
Tuna fish and mayonnaise
Hershey bars and grapefruit in the cart
We're stocking up her larder
But why I'm really there
Is to hold my mother in my heart

I remember goin' to the grocery with my Mom
I was sittin' in the cart - we rolled along
I produced some chatter
Momma hummed a song
Goin' to the grocery with my Mom

But the road leads on –
That's life's plan
And a little boy
Becomes an old man –
Goin' to the grocery without Mom

Yes, the road leads on
And so do we
And what once was
Is used to be

But although she's gone
I will always be
Goin' to the grocery with my Mom
Goin' to the grocery with my Mom
Goin' to the grocery with my Mom

http://www.youtube.com/watch?v=9dSP0hh0g00
Search: # 77 Goin' to the Grocery with My Mom

I'll Fly Away

I'll fly away beyond the sky
Beyond the sun – the time has come
I'll fly away

I'll spread my wings a dove of peace
And coo a song of sweet release
I'll fly away

Beyond the sky, beyond the Moon
Beyond the music of the Spheres
Beyond the Stars, beyond all tears
I'll fly away

Into the air I'll spread my wings
And without care do wondrous things
I'll fly away

Into the Night I will take flight
And without Rage but with Delight
I'll leave this cage
I'll fly away

I'll fly away

http://www.youtube.com/watch?v=G8H4yG317bA
Search: Uke Man "I'll Fly Away"

I Believe in Jesus

Oh, I believe, I believe in you, Jesus
Jesus can you believe in me?

He was born in Bethlehem and raised in Galilee
And all it was for was to nail him on a tree
Oh, Jesus can you believe in me?

Well, he went out lookin' for fishermen
Said, "Come on boys! We're gonna fish for men
and together we can change the world"

Then he sat on his ass and he rode into town
Why's everybody tryin' to put him down
sayin' "No long-haired hippie freaks need apply"

Oh, I believe, I believe in you, Jesus
Jesus can you believe in me?

Then he took 'em all to his Last Supper
and everybody thought it was gonna be an upper
'til he told 'em one would betray and another deny

Then he took 'em out to Gethsemane
and said, "Who's gonna stay up and pray with me?"
and they all fell asleep in a minute or two

He was kneelin' down there on the ground
blood was oozin' from his pores all around
He even cried out to his Daddy for some help

He said, "Daddy, I'm doin' the best that I can. I know I'm God
but I'm also a man; so if you can, please take this cup from me"

Oh, I believe, I believe in you, Jesus
Jesus can you believe in me?

Hey there, Mister, listen to this
Judas came up and betrayed him with a kiss
and they locked him up and hauled him away

But before they did, Peter pulled his sword
said, "I'm gonna cut off an ear for the Lord"
But Jesus just put that ear right back on

Then they took him to Pilate, the man from Rome
who said, "Jesus Christ, where is your home?"
He said, "My home is not of this world"

He says, "Jesus Christ I'll give you anything you choose,
all you gotta say's you're not King of the Jews !
Oh, Jesus! We're gonna crucify you!"

Well, just like always, we showed him who's boss
took him and nailed him up on a cross
Oh, Jesus   Oh Jesus!!

He was born in Bethlehem and raised in Galilee
And all it was for was to nail him on a tree
Oh, Jesus can you believe in me?
Oh, Jesus can you believe in me?

http://www.youtube.com/watch?v=BKXbcu6ZJxo
Search: # 76 - "I Believe in Jesus" - Ty & the Uke Man

Jesus on the Mainline

I know a lot of people who
talk to God,
and He answers them back,
especially if they
"pray on it."

One guy told me
he could get 300 people,
at the drop of a hat,
to *pray on it* with me.
That should improve the odds
don't you think.

It's sort of funny though.
With all the modern technology,
no one ever records their conversations
or snaps a picture.
Maybe God is shy or feels
he needs more practice
before appearing publicly.

I understand that He
generally tells my friends
what they want to hear,
which seems a little odd.

It's almost as if they were talking to
a politician . . . or
             . . . to themselves,

and you know what they say about that.

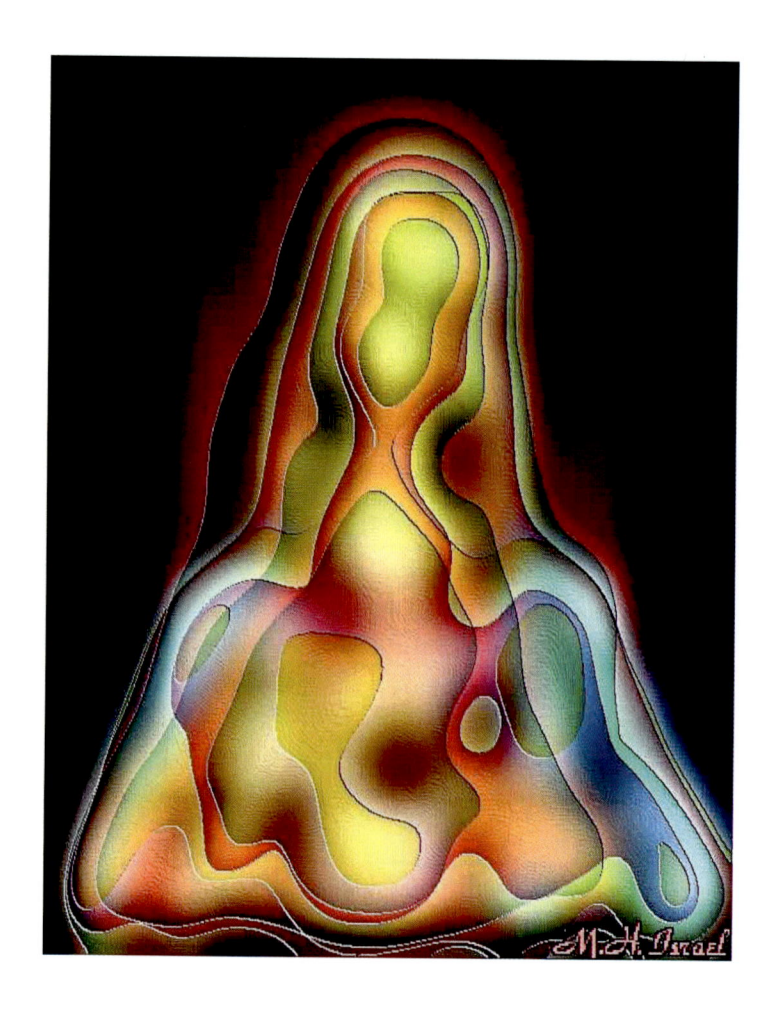

Samson Was a Man

There was a Little Man and he had a little Plan
And that's how civilization began

Had some boys carry him all around
So his little tiny feet never touched the ground

He gave some weapons to a select few
And everything he said we all had to do

Then he screwed all the luscious, nubile babes
And made all the rest of us his virtual slaves

He designated some to be his priests
And all they would talk about was the beast

They tried to make us worry 'bout our soul
To help with the Little Man's control

But Samson was a man and he tore the Temple down
Samson was a man and he tore the Temple down
Samson was a man and he tore the Temple down
Left all that marble lyin' on the ground

It didn't fit the Little Man's Plan
To find out Samson was a man
But Samson was a man and he tore the Temple down
Left the Little Man lyin' on the ground

Think about the Little Man lyin' on the ground
After Samson tore the Temple down
Little Man, Little Man, don't you cry
We're all here just to wave bye-bye

Samson was a man and he tore the temple down
Samson was a man and he tore the temple down
Left all that marble lyin' on the ground

http://www.youtube.com/watch?v=sWxReuzGcpQ
Search: # 97 Samson Was a Man

John Kasich

John Kasich
the old man with the baby face

(he loves Jesus, you see)

can bullshit in his sleep
with the smooth certainty of one
who spews Biblical truth
from both sides of his mouth

Raised Catholic, he found Jesus
on the road to Damtaxes
and was born again

anointed with snake oil.

Tower in the Sky

When you were young you always said
You'd build a Tower to the Sky
Now you're grown and it's begun
This tower to the Sky

And you believe that when it's done
We'll all bow down to you
And in your pride and certainty
you know that it is true

But you know not what you do

You are not the only one
Living here beneath the sun
And when your tower's built and done
We'll live beneath its shadow and its gloom

Will you crush our bones for mortar
To build your tower to the sky
Will you lay your bricks upon our hearts
To build your tower to the sky

Will you sell the children
And their mothers too?

To build your tower in the sky
Is there nothing you won't do?
There in your Penthouse in the sky
Safe from all your fears
You've closed your heart and shut your eyes
To all our pain and all our tears

You know not what you do

I'll not be the only one
In mourning here upon the ground
And when your tower's built and done
We'll tear your tower down

No, I'll not be the only one
Dark and huddled on the ground
To rise up to the blessed sun
And tear your tower down
We'll tear your tower down.

http://www.youtube.com/watch?v=SgG7K4sQTl0
Search: # 16 - "Tower in the Sky" (The John Kasich Memorial Tower of Babel)

Gov. Johnny Kasich's Nightmare Cafe

Ladies and gentlemen, I welcome you today
To Gov. Johnny Kasich's Nightmare Cafe

There is no entry fee. Nobody needs to pay
Except for Lehman Brothers should they show up here today

And you'll notice Rupert Murdock isn't here
And you won't see Glenn Beck over there swilling beer
They and Rush Limbaugh are afraid to come near
Gov. Johnny Kasich's Nightmare Cafe

But Militia Men and Tea Baggers
You need not stay away Uke Man has a cure for you
Right here in Gov. Johnny Kasich's Nightmare Cafe

We'll not board Kasich's bus!! We'll drag his bus to Hell
Where he can chat with Satan whom he has served so well
His nasty arrogance is banned from here today

Welcome, welcome, welcome, welcome, welcome
To Gov. Johnny Kasich's Nightmare Cafe

http://www.youtube.com/watch?v=BjNoZxqP5hA   Search: # 34 Governor Johnny Kasich's Nightmare Cafe !

Bleed Blues

If you've got what you want
you think you've got what you need
If you've got what you need
you think you don't have to bleed

But everybody's got to bleed
it's the truth, yes indeed
There ain't no bandaid for the problem
everybody's got to bleed

And we're gonna bleed
yeah, we're gonna bleed
Gonna bleed all over
yes indeed

Yeah, we're gonna bleed
all over the place
Gonna bleed on the earth
gonna bleed in outer space

Yeah, we're gonna bleed
it's a God-given need
I hope there ain't no confusion
'cause all of us gonna need a
transfusion

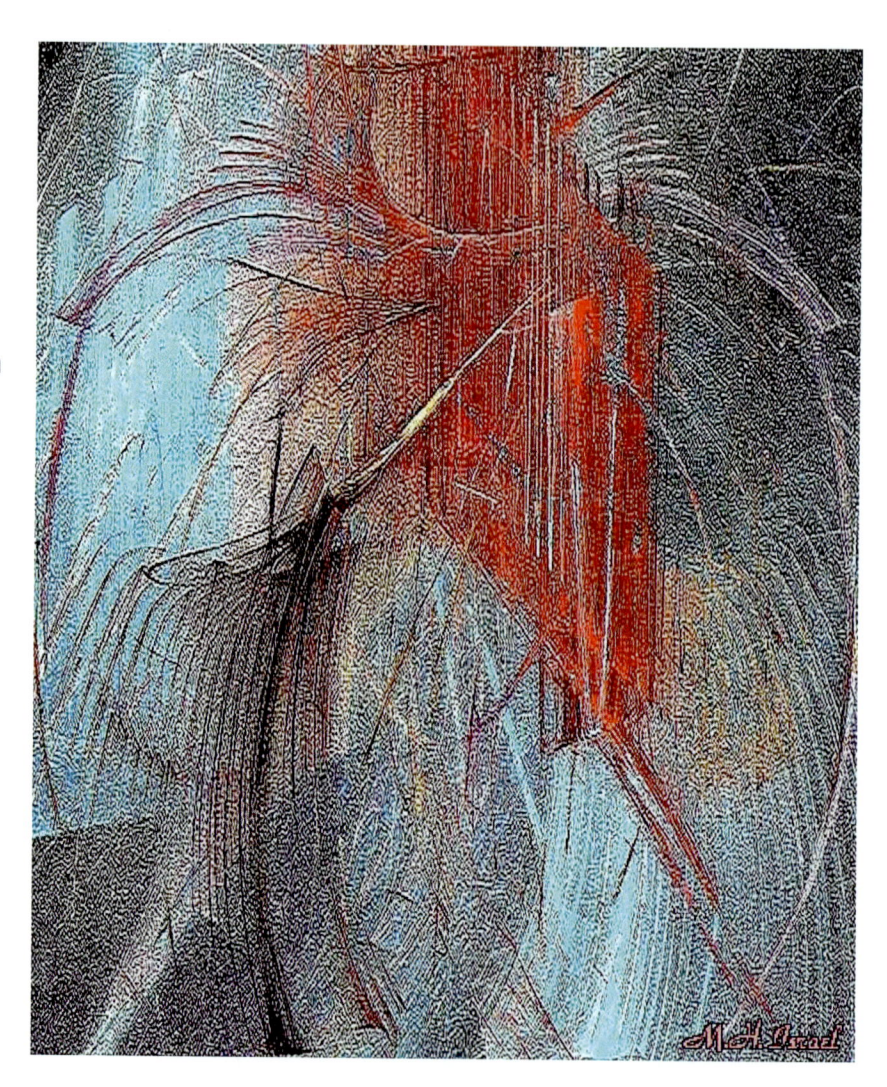

http://www.youtube.com/watch?v=YMM9BdDTZno
Search: # 12 - Khabu & the Uke Man - Bleed Blues - October 08

Wish I

Wish I, wish I, wish I could,
Live forever, live forever, here with you.
Wish I, wish I, wish I could,
Do everything you want me to
Be everything and more for you,
I wish I could,
But it's too late; it's too late for me.

Wish I, wish I, wish I could,
Make all your dreams come true
Be everything and more for you,
I wish I could, but it's too late,
It's too late for me.

    I've done everything I can
    To be your one true lovin' man,
    And I'd do it all again,
    But it's too late; it's too late for me.

Wish I, wish I, wish I could,
Live forever, live forever here with you.
Wish I, wish I, wish I could,
Make all your dreams come true
Do everything you want me to,
I wish I could
But it's too late; it's too late for me.

    I've done everything I can
    To be your one true lovin' man,
    And I'd do it all again,
    But it's too late; it's too late for me.

    Oh . . . it's too late for me.

    http://www.youtube.com/watch?v=s7SYF4k-XAg
    Search: Ukulele Man - "Wish I"

Sorry

I'm sorry for being a man.
Women are such tender flowers that
We bruise them with our embrace.

Men are practical and open.
Women bloom in the ether
And wonder what our callouses portend.

We are drawn to their beauty and their fragility
And they long, in their turn,
For our touch.

Yet it seems it is not meant to be
Though it most certainly shall
Even though it makes a chaos out of hoping
For the happy medium.

I'm sorry for being a man.
But I would not be a woman either.
Rather, I would crush God
For his little joke -
And make men and women one.

Better Tomorrow

I am a man - I do the best I can
even though it may bring me sorrow
I am a man - do the best I can
and I'll do better tomorrow

because I've got a woman
she treats me good
the way that a woman knows that she should,
and I'm gonna be so much better tomorrow

I am a man - I do the best I can
even though it may bring me sorrow
I am a man - do the best I can
and I'll do better tomorrow

because I've got a woman
she treats me right
makes love to me every day and night
and I'm gonna be so much better tomorrow

I'm gonna be so much better tomorrow

http://www.youtube.com/watch?v=jJfVGEGkjiU
Search: # 112 - Better Tomorrow

Goodbye Larry's

Goodbye, Larry's; I hate to see you go
Goodbye, Larry's, goodbye
You've been around forever
As far as I know
Oh, Larry's I hate to see you go

You've always been a part of me
Seems almost like Family
Now you've up and gone away
But we'll meet up again someday

Goodbye, Larry's; I hate to see you go
Goodbye, Larry's, goodbye

Batman came and did his thing
But now where's Batman gonna sing?
Goodbye, Larry's, goodbye

Emily says nothing Gold can stay
And today you've up and gone away
Goodbye, Larry's, goodbye

You knew me way back when
We've been friends since then
And though all good things must finally end
we'll meet again as friends

I'll bring my band; we'll sing and play
Maybe in hell, but that's ok
Goodbye, Larry's, goodbye

And if it's in hell, well, I don't care
There's no Republicans or Frat boys there
Goodbye, Larry's, goodbye

Goodbye, Larry's, I hate to see you go
You know I'm gonna miss you so

There must be something in my eye
Or maybe I'm just gonna cry
Goodbye, Larry's, goodbye
Goodbye, Larry's, goodbye

http://www.youtube.com/watch?v=2sGAAXLWQI4
Search: Larry's Finished Tom Harker #26

A Walk in the Park

Walkin' in circles
Ain't goin' nowhere
Talkin' to the walls
And they don't care
Suckin' in the air hangin' round my head
and lyin' to my empty bed

    Is there a way out of here
    To somewhere else Far or Near
    It's gotta be better there than here
    I guess I should
    Take a Walk in the Park

Sittin' on the porch
No place to go
Sittin' on the porch
Watchin' grass grow
All my wild oats done already been sowed
Maybe I should take a walk in the park

There goes Joe and Edna; her dress is tore
Joe beats that girl; she comes back for more
He's the man that she adores
I think I'll go inside and shut the door

    There must be a way out of here
    To somewhere else Far or Near
    Somewhere else, better than here
    Maybe I'll go
    Take a Walk in the Park

Well, I went down to the Dollar Store
Found the Rev. goin' on about Dinosaurs
Said on Sundays he needs to see me more
I done that once   but not no more
A cold day in hell when I walk through his door
I'd rather take a walk in the Park

Stopped for a drink at Shifty's bar
Mike said, "The Park ain't *that* far,
Have a few beers an' shed a few tears.
She's been gone now how many years?
You can always take your walk in the Park"

Ol' Norm speaks up, "Come on I'll take you in my car"
A 57 Chevy – Norm's a star
But I say, "Thanks, I gotta stay right here
Until I've had a few more beers
Then I'll take my walk in the park"

>Yeah, I'm gonna sit right here
>Until I've raised a few more beers
>To your sweet memory, My Dear
>Then I'll take our walk in the Park

Sit on the bench
Feed the pigeons and squirrels
Watch the boys chasin' after the girls
If you should come by, we can give it a whirl
And take a walk in the park

>Yeah, there's a way out of here
>Evening's arrived and night draws near
>So, hold my hand and hold me near
>And we'll take our Walk in the Park

>So, hold my hand once more my dear
>Hold my hand and hold me near
>And we'll take our Walk in the Park

>And
>steal a kiss
>in the dark

http://www.youtube.com/watch?v=psBdhGst6Ss&feature=youtu.be
Search: # 114 - A Walk in the Park

Vi

There is a look of death
when one is old enough
and worn enough,

and I have seen it.

I will see it again, I think,
if violence and accident
should pass me by.

It is an awful look,
But embrace it
I will.

Ashes to Ashes

Under the ancient cedars
Howard was laid to rest

a little cardboard mailing box with tape
and mailing address.

Ashes to ashes, dust to dust

Cajun cremation / Midwestern interment
under the ancient cedars.

Dr. Jekyll Had Something to Hide

Dr. Jekyll came to my little town
Opened up a practice and went on his rounds
We all said that he looked OK
but we knew he had something to hide

Never joined Kiwanis, and he wasn't an Elk
Had strange tastes in music; didn't like Lawrence Welk
Wasn't a Mason, and he didn't golf
And he used a wicked-lookin' knife on the warts he cut off

 Well, down at the Church you could hear us talk
 And we'd write up our thoughts with the Christian-Ed chalk
 And we'd tell everybody and we'd say it with pride
 Dr. Jekyll had something to hide

We said he was Jewish; said he was gay
Said it was wrong what he asked us to pay
Said we'd all be sorry some day
'Cause Dr. Jekyll had something to hide

 Oh, oh, oh

So, we took our torches, a thousand points of light
And we took our pitchforks, ready for a fight
And we visited him in the middle of the night
To see what Dr. Jekyll had to hide

And we rousted him out when we got there
He had sleep in his eyes and disheveled hair
"Father in heaven," Dr. Jekyll cried
A sure sign he had something to hide

So we tied him up, hands and feet
And crowned him king with a holly wreath
Then we beat him to death right there in the street
Now who's got something to hide

 Oh, oh, oh

Now down at the Chamber you can still hear us talk
And we write up our plans with the Rotary's chalk
And we tell everybody our town is peaceful and calm
And we urge you to move here with nary a qualm
And we tell everybody, and we say it with pride
Our little town has nothing to hide

Search: # 102 - Dr Jekyll Had Something to Hide
http://www.youtube.com/watch?v=RG-1dEYRQAM

Skinhead Arisin'

I see a Skinhead arisin' under a blood-red moon
I see a Skinhead arisin' Apocalypse must be comin' soon
I see Swastikas a'growin, thick as hair upon a young man's head
I hear the chorus of the Living transcribed to Dirges for the Dead

    Ronald Reagan didn't care except about his perfect hair
    But I guess we all helped to put him there
    Oh, Ronald Reagan didn't care

I hear the Devil's music playin' – sawin' out the harmonies of hell
I hear the politicians sayin' "Everything's just fine; it's really swell"
I see a Skinhead arisin' – I hear the Devil's merry tune
I see a Skinhead arisin' – castin' darkness down upon the Noon

    Ronald Reagan didn't care except about his perfect hair
    But I guess we all helped to put him there
    Oh, Ronald Reagan didn't care

I hear the Storm Troopers marching, stomping out the rhythms of War
I hear the lurid laughing of Satan consorting with his whore
I see the Cross of Jesus lyin' rusty there upon the ground
I hear the screamin' of the Children cryin' out for Justice as they drown

    Ronald Reagan didn't care. Hello, is there anyone out there?
    Don't you think it's time we tried to share?
    Does anybody really care?

Search:# 113 - Skinhead Arisin'
http://www.youtube.com/watch?v=Zyzcf-cd8yM&feature=youtu.be

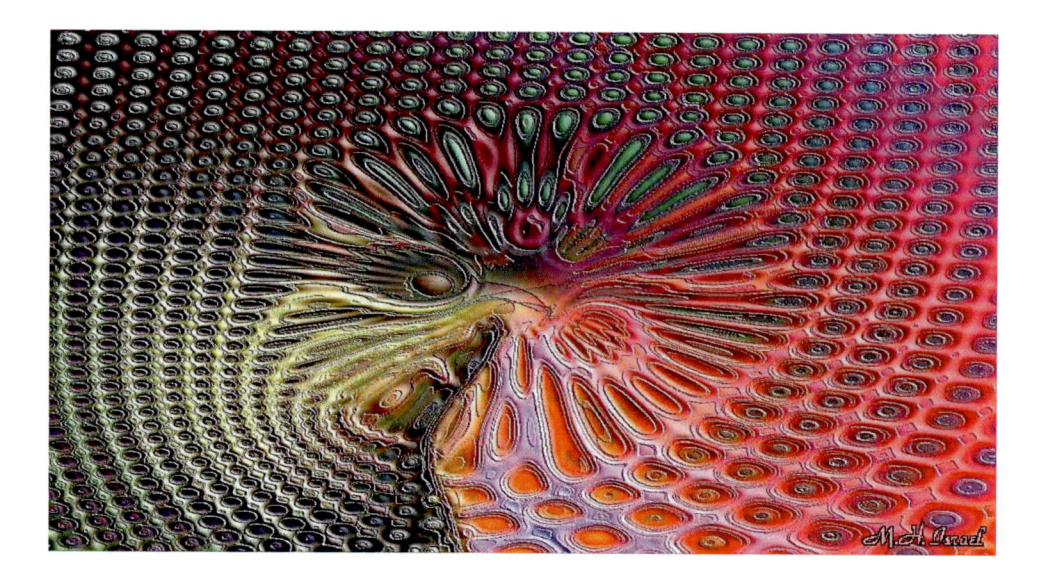

Down On the Farm

Chewing our cuds, rolling our eyes, lolling beneath cardboard, empty blue skies - indolent Holsteins!
No shades of gray! We're all black and white, baking cow pies all day; spewing volumes of
methane - with no words to say.

And they milk us and breed us until one fine day when it's time for the knacker to take us away,
and then we are ground beef and fed to their dogs, middle-class Holsteins (better off than the
hogs who are slaughtered much sooner and eaten with pride by the fork-wielding Man who has
Dog on his side).

Sure, they milk us and skin us and grind us up well, but forever *that* truth is forbidden to tell.
Deny it, suppress it, hide it with stealth. Tell it to no one not even yourself.

. . . .

On rain-glazed white chickens so much can depend when the wheelbarrow red revolves once
again and hatches a prophet who demands that we speak, and sings out that *courage* is what
we must seek! And prods us on to-it with the strength of his beak! Inherit the wind – not the
earth – if you're meek.

. . . .

Bovinish beatitudes, dairy farm platitudes - but Mr. Jones' attitudes have Dog on their side.
Productivity's up, supply and demand; "Supply more with less!" is Jones's command.
The Cow Jones Industrials and the Nazduck are grand; so shut up and kneel and give Dog a
hand.

Pork bellies are up and Capital gains - while the manor-born feed on our bodies and brains.
And Dog preaches on in his saccharine tones, speaking down to us from his pulpit of bones of
the sweet, blessed oil that's squeezed from our blood, as we "Moooo" our "Amen's" and plod
on through the mud.

We are the hollow cows, guts filled with straw! Cowardly lions eating collard greens - raw!
Self-blinded fools marching into the maw of Dog and country and the Rule of Law. "Damn the
torpedoes; full speed ahead; salute the flag or you too could be dead." See not what they did;
just hear what they said. Yeah, the blood's on *their* hands, but the cost's on *our* heads!

. . . .

And so, the prophet demands that we speak, and sings out that *courage* is what we must seek!
So stand up and curse and – finally – speak! Spit out your cud;
awake from the dream; banish the nightmare; and stand up and scream!
Banish the nightmare; and stand up and scream!

Got Myself a Parrot

Well, I got myself a parrot
And bought her a fancy cage

And got a copy of the *Dispatch*
Turned to the Editorial Page

I put 'em all together
Watched my Parrot shake her feathers
And do what any self-respecting bird would do

She shit on the Wolf Man
She shit on the Wolf Man
Do unto him as he's done to me and you

Now I've lived just about all my life
Right here in Columbus town

And every time I pick it up
The *Dispatch* puts me down

They'd like to deny it,
but it's plain to see

It's everything for the Wolf Man
To hell with you and me

So, get yourself a parrot
And buy her a fancy cage

And get a copy of the *Dispatch*
Turned to the Editorial Page

Put 'em all together
and watched your Parrot shake her feathers
And do what any self-respecting bird would do

She'll shit on the Wolf Man
She'll shit on the Wolf Man
Do unto him as he's done to me and you!!

http://www.youtube.com/watch?v=ZluxD26DhJ0
Search: # 45 - Got Myself a Parrot

Fascist Girl

Come on baby, give me a whirl
Won't you be my fascist girl?
Come on baby, give me a try
I wanna be your fascist guy
We can burn our torches bright
And make a thousand points of light
Come on baby and be my fascist girl

I'm so happy that I am so filthy rich
I can be an aristocrat
and you can be my bitch
We can paint a swastika on our BMW
come on baby and be my fascist girl

Come on baby, we can spend our days
bashing lesbians and gays
At night we can get our kicks
harassing Jews and Catholics
we can leave a foreigner
bleeding on the corner
come on baby and be my fascist girl

We'll surely get our pictures
In *The ColumbusDispatch*
Citizen's award for removing trash
Baby can't you feel the thrill of
Rubbing shoulders with George Will
Come on baby and be my fascist girl

Oh fascist girl you are the best
With the tattoo of Reagan on your breast

Come on baby, join the master race
Limbaugh's saving you a place
And I know you'll like my wienie
Looks a lot like Mussolini
Come on baby and be my fascist girl
Oh, yeah, come on baby and be my fascist girl

http://www.youtube.com/watch?v=_532NlapoKo
Search: "Fascist Girl / From an Undisclosed Location"

Going Postal

Going postal
it's Bi-coastal
it's Bi-polar
it's Disorder

Tell the
Pollster
Check my
Holster

Revolution's
Resolution
The solution:
Institution

Permutation
Of the nation
Inspiration
Perspiration

It's just sweat
(Whatcha get!!)
Just regret !
For whatcha et

democratic
Prophylactic
Psycho
somatic & didactic

Eat my shorts
File your torts
Kangaroooo me
In your courts

Hang me
Dang me
Re-a-rang me
Knife me
Wife me
End of life me

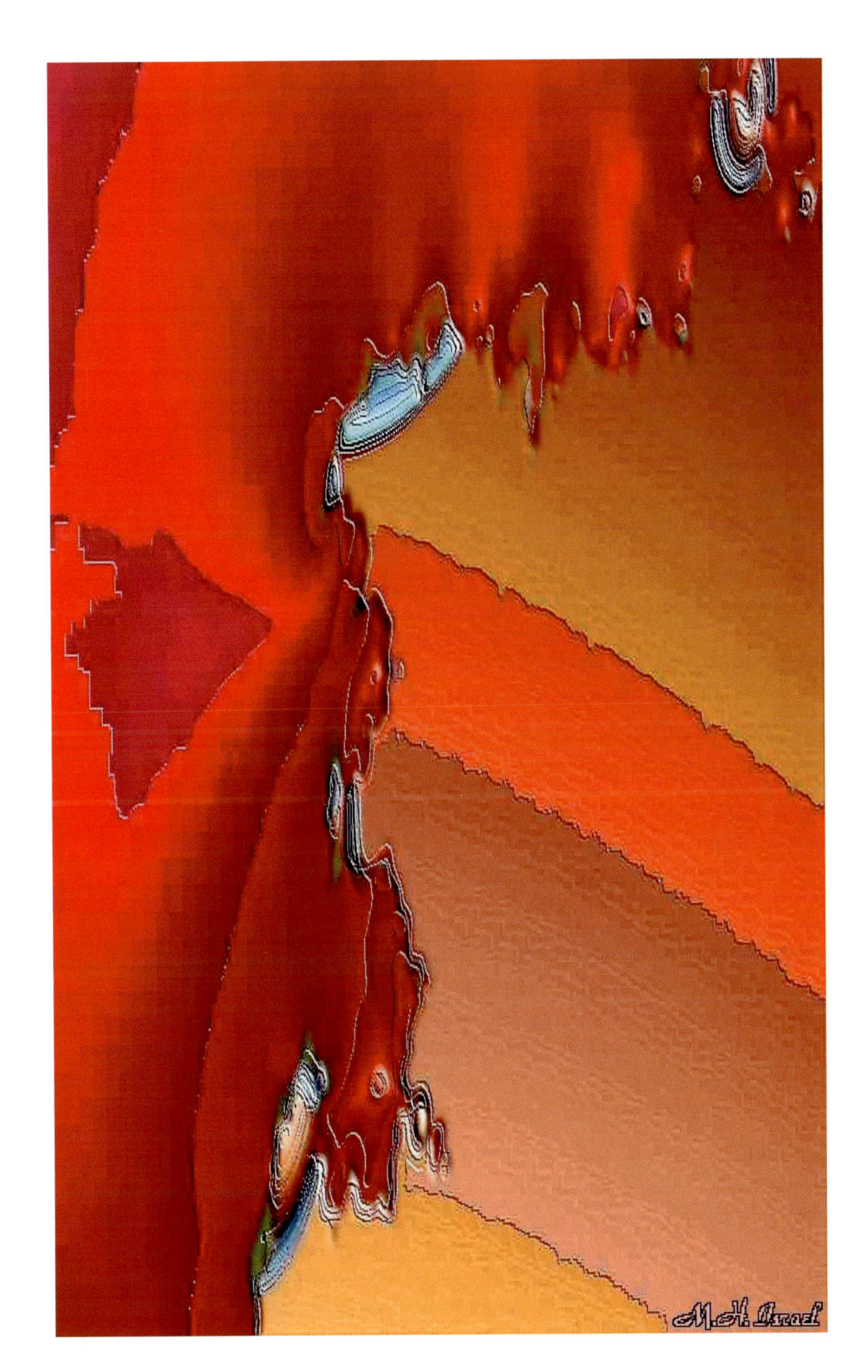

Burn me
Spurn me
Non-return me

Date me
Hate me
& Blue Plate me

Tell me
Sell me
Axe-Man fell me

I am going
Ain't it showing?
Can't you feel the undertowing?

Postal
Postal
Postal
Postal

Bang!
Bang!
Ba-a-a-a-a-a-a-a-a-a-a-n-g !!!

I Wantta Get Off

Fuck the world! I wantta get off
And commiserate with old Bob Goff.
Sit an' masturbate the live-long day
An' think 'bout how to make 'em pay,

Th' dumb sumbitches that prance around
Thinkin' their feet don't touch the ground,
Grindin' other fellahs down
Turnin' a man . . . into a clown!

Fuck the world! That's what I said!
I got a list o' who should be dead.
Buy me a gun and have some fun!
Kill 'em dead! Every - single - fucking - one!!

I've Had Enough of Death

I've had enough of Death
and old Sam Donaldson
(before they swept him out the door)
(before we had this fucking war)
Saying: ***"If we go to Iraq once more,
we should kill him –***

***this** time !!"*

I'm tired of the handsome, empty heads
who took Sam's place
demanding death, with earnest face:
"Death death death –
We killed some more today!!
Death to terror – bombs away
Shock and awe!
Let us pray."

I'm tired, too, of the Monkey Man who had a plan –
long before his term began - to kill Saddam and then Iran –
"Dead or alive" - So cock sure,
Cloaked inside his bloated pride.

Bring 'em on; let's have some fun!!
Kill the bastards, every one;
Liberty, you see, is on the move
Starbucks – Wal-Mart – Jiffy Lube.

The sacred Market has decreed
who will live and who will bleed,
Who will prosper, who will breathe,
Who will die and who will grieve.

Death, destruction, grief, and rubble
Profiteers earn
and oil …
bubble.

- - -

Thrice the brindled cat hath mewed
Thrice and once the hedgepig whined
The Holy Writ is misconstrued
The best of us have lost our minds.
And by the pricking of my thumbs,
Much that's wicked has been done.

- - -

So, bring 'em on; let's have some fun !!!!!
Kill the bastards, every one;
Yeah! kill the bastards, every one;

Kill us all !!! Everyone !!!

(when **all** are dead
our show is done)

Intelligent Design, My Ass!!

I'm tired of God. Enough of Him! **Him** & his *crap*!

Yeah! It was *good ol' God* when I was small -
I'd fall asleep - sitting on his lap
But after the nap, it was *"Up against the Wall!!"*

Yeah! and He strutted around all holier than thou
(as if He really *knew* thou then
As if he even knows thou *NOW*) !

Yeah, with God all things are possible!!!
But not in Ohio!! Not on the earth!!

Not while you're *ALIVE* !! Not after your *BIRTH*, but after your *DEATH* !!
That's when you're *WITH* god!!!
After you're *DEAD*!!
First MAN must *DIE* and *THEN* get ahead!

But you say *GOD's* with you now!!!?? Well send him over here! Let the deity speak; and I'll buy him a beer!

Hey! Let's hear it for GOD!! Let's give him a hand!!!
Hey bartender! a beer! And strike up the band.

   *   *   *

What?! Oh, he's caught in traffic somewhere in the land.

The Omnipotent's caught up in a Grand traffic Jam ??
as Intelligently Designed in his Grand Master Plan ??
Predestined, I guess, from before the first days –
To show off his might in ever new ways.

But alas, that old question is answered, to wit:
can he make a heavy stone he cannot lift?

The answer's "Yes!" since He isn't here!
(and, don't hold your breath!
and forget about the beer)

A stone so heavy he cannot lift it;
Traffic so snarled he cannot exit.

See! Even God can't do everything right

Not in Ohio -   at least not tonight!
But all is not lost; we can still trust the Boss
In God We *still* Trust. Isn't that right?

The Federal Bureau of Graven Images
vouches for him – and always will.
They say so in writing - on the dollar bill,
and if You don't trust the Dollar; well, who the hell will?

But it's not the same for 'telligent Design !
Unless the Almighty is out of his mind.

Ebola, AIDS, avian flu, malaria, cholera, and TB too –
Does any of that sound smart to you?

He made man in His image
How wise was that?
If I look like God!
Then He's old, bald, and fat;
And the people around us throughout all our days
Reflect on God too - in unflattering ways.

He's stupid and jealous and spiteful and mean
Writes "YAWEH" in the snow when he vents his spleen.

He sends us to Hell and won't let us leave,
This creator of DEATH who tries to blame Eve -
But he made HER, and he made the TREE!
And He made Cain and you and me!

Well, he fucked up, didn't he!!
He fucked up, yes sir-eee!

After all, WE're the "ZENITH of his creation"
The "culmination of Intelligent Design"
Especially the citizens of THIS great nation
Pristine and pure and noble and kind.
Who believes THAT ???????
The deaf, dumb, and blind !!!!!!!!!!!!

Remember, Man, that thou art dust and to dust
Thou shalt return.

No, we ain't that much, not worth the fuss
And neither is God.
I'm tired of God
And he's damned tired of us.

Sometimes I Wonder

Sometimes I wonder, sometimes I wonder
How I've lived 'til now and come here to this place.

I feel the walls closin' in around me
It's never happened to me before.
I feel the walls closin' in around me
Can you open up a door?

Always done what I'm supposed to
Always done what's right.
Then why's the sun goin' down on me
Why's this place look like night?

See the road a'stretchin' out in front of me,
Don't know where it goes to
See the road a'stretchin' out in front of me,
Can I walk it with you?

Don't believe in Heaven; don't believe in Hell
And I don't believe I'm doin' so well
Here in this place.

I feel the walls closin' in around me
It's never happened to me before.
I feel the walls closin' in around me
Can you open up a door?

Don't believe in Heaven; don't believe in Hell
And I don't believe I'm doin' so well
Here in this place.

I think I'll take my problems somewhere else
Think I'll take them there today.
I think I'll take my problems somewhere else
Can you show me the way?

Sometimes I wonder, sometimes I wonder
How I've lived 'til now & come here to this place,
Here to this place.

http://www.youtube.com/watch?v=ym8fodbMYaA
Search: Uke Man Sometimes I Wonder

Do You Know

Do you know which way to go
If you do, won't you show me
Do you know which way to go
If you do, won't you take me there

I can't make it on my own
I can't walk this world alone
So, if you would won't you
please take me home with you

Can you see the good in me
If you can, won't you tell me
Can you hear I need you near
Lend an ear and I'll tell you

I can't make it on my own
I can't walk this world alone
So, if you would won't you
please take me home with you

Do you know if I'm your beaux
If you do, won't you tell me so
Does that sigh mean I'm your guy
If it does, won't you hold me tight

I can't make it on my own
I can't walk this world alone
So, if you would won't you
please take me home with you

I think I know which way to go
Hold my hand and I'll take you there.
Take my hand, I'll be your man
We'll walk this land, together

We can make it, you and me
Have a home and raise a family
Paint the house and plant a little tree, you and me
Oh so happy we will be, you and me
Oh so happy we will be
you and me

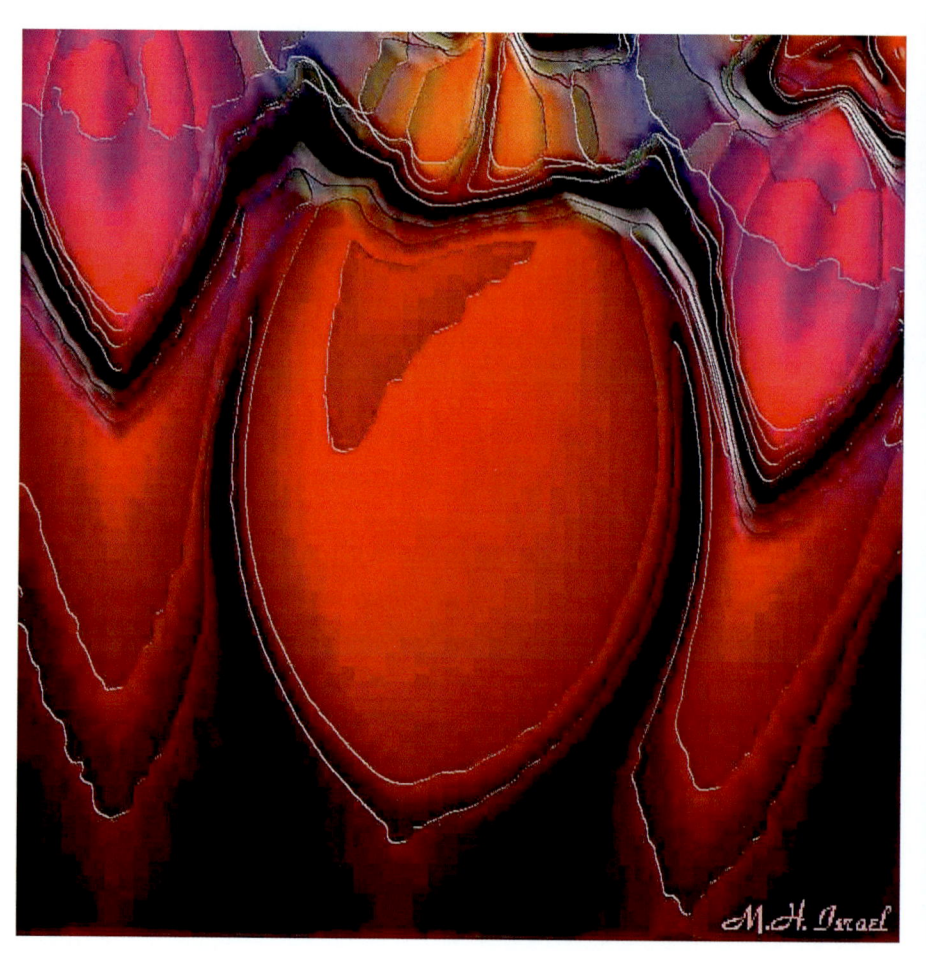

http://www.youtube.com/watch?v=9HyKWCkkU0Q
Search: # 33 - Do You Know Tom Harker

Hard Drinkin' Mama

She's my hard-drinkin' baby; she's quite a lady
And I'm her hard-drinkin' man

We may look funny and we ain't got much money
But we're doin' the best that we can

We go the bars but they treat us like stars
And everyone there knows our name

She's my hard-drinkin' baby, and I don't mean maybe
She keeps me from going insane

She's my hard-drinkin' girlie; she's a mite squirrely
But she's got a bright bushy tail

And under the covers we're like two young lovers
Oh lord, how we moan and we wail

She's my hard-drinkin' Mama; she likes my salama
And I like the things she can do

She's my hard-drinkin' baby, and I don't mean maybe
I'm glad she's with me not with you

And when we go drinkin' it gets me to thinkin'
How lucky I am to have her
She's my hard-drinkin' baby; she's quite a Lady for sure
She's my hard-drinkin' baby; she's quite a Lady for sure

http://www.youtube.com/watch?v=bjVLw-ZQAoY
Search: # 51 Hard-Drinkin' Mama at Larry's in the dark

Moonshine

Oh the sun comes up in the mornin'
and shines down on the earth
Well, at least it has every day
since the day of my birth

But then the moon comes out in the evenin'
and starts to shine
I hope you've had a little moonshine in your life;
I've had a bit in mine.

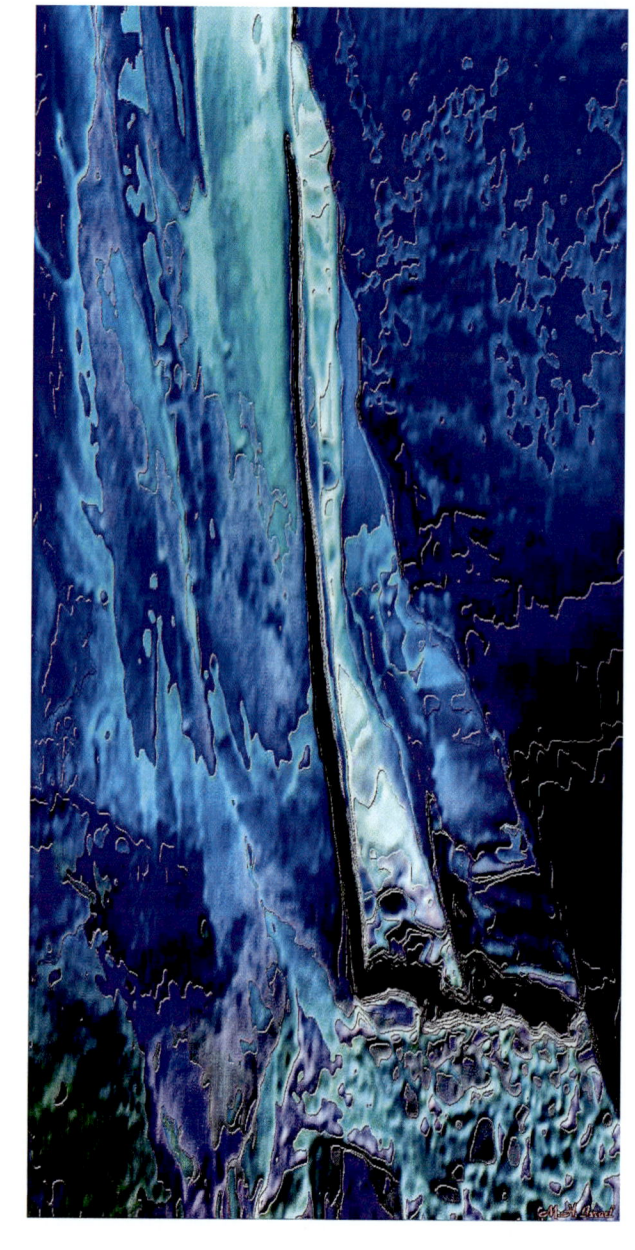

And the Moon shines down on the corner
and makes us all feel good
Oh, the Moon shines down on the corner
but it makes it hard to get up
in the mornin' like we should.

Oh the sun comes up in the mornin'
so we can earn our pay
And he shines and watches
as we work all through the day
But then the Moon comes out in the evenin'
and has her say
And she shines and shines 'n' shines
our troubles all away.

And the Moon shines down on the corner
and makes us feel all right
Oh, the Moon shines down on the corner
It's gonna shine all night

Oh the sun comes up in the mornin' and shines down on the world
And it warms us all, men, women, boys, and girls.
But the Moon shines warmer than the sun can ever do
So here's another round for everyone, and here's to me and you.

And the Moon shines down on the corner and makes us feel all right
Oh, the Moon shines down on you and me
It's gonna shine all night

Oh the sun comes up in the mornin' and shines down on the earth
Well, at least it has every day since the day of my birth

But then the moon comes out in the evenin' and starts to shine
I hope you've had a little moonshine in your life
I've had a bit in mine

http://www.youtube.com/watch?v=sEOSjerRtWs&feature=youtu.be
Search: # 107 - Moonshine

Pea-Green Boat

Why don't we just float away
Why don't we leave to day
We'll float along through tangerine skies
you and I

In my beautiful pea-green boat

The Owl & the Pussycat
they'll both be there
Owl with his wisdom
and Pussy with her devil-may-care
We'll sing a love song as we float along
you and I

in my beautiful pea-green boat

I'll be the Owl
and give you my horny stare
You can be Pussy
and you'll do your share

We'll be alright
as we dance through the night
by the light of the moon

in my beautiful pea-green boat

    Why don't we just float away
    sail for a year and a day
    Lord knows we've had our dues to pay
    Now it's time to play

in my beautiful pea-green boat

Why don't we just float away
Why don't we leave today
We'll be alright as we float through the night
and the tangerine skies
by the light of the moon
of the silvery moon

In my beautiful pea-green boat

    http://www.youtube.com/watch?v=X6bw1lFgUUY
    search: #73 - Pea Green Boat - Englishman John's Reunion:

Until the End of Love

I look into your eyes and you look into mine
And you tell me that you'll love me 'til the end of time

You look into my eyes and I look into yours
And the kitten on your lap oh how sweetly she purrs

I look into your eyes and you look into mine
And I tell you that I'll love you until the end of time

But the World will do what it will do
The World can neither love nor be true

So, let the World do what it will do
As long as I have you to love me until the end of time

I look into your eyes and you look into mine
And you tell me that you'll love me 'til the end of time

And the World can go away for all that I care
As long as you are there in your rocking chair
To love me until the end of time

And though, even time can end – no time to start again
It is written: Time can't end
until the end of Love

Time can't end until the end of Love

So, hold me in your arms
and I'll hold you in mine

Unending love can make time run
Our love will make time run –

Until the end of time

http://www.youtube.com/watch?v=Pv9lxfdkkiM
Search: # 99 Until the End of Love

Play My Ukulele Forever

When we were young, the days were long
Day followed after day

We thought they would last forever
But someday the piper must be paid

And I can't play my ukulele forever
That's why I'm playin' it today

And I can't sing my songs forever
So I'll just sing and play for you today

You know how much I love you
You know how much I care
You know how much I need you
And the love we share

But I can't play my ukulele forever
So I'll just sing and play for you today

You know how much I love you
You know how much I care
You know how much I need you
And the love we share

But I can't play my ukulele forever
That's why I'm playin' it today
And I can't sing my songs forever
So I'll just sing and play for you today

I'll just sing and play for you today

http://www.youtube.com/watch?v=Zt2onjgm3zw
Search: # 5 - Play My Ukulele - with Trumpet

Out There Somewhere

Out there – way, way out there
There's a place for me

Out there – way, way out there
There's a land that's real and true and free

Let me take you down cause I'm going to
Somewhere where there's nothing to get hung about
Somewhere way, way out there

Where all the cops have wooden legs
And the lemonade brooks and the popcorn cooks all day
Where pretty nurses sell poppies on Penny Lane
And the U.S. mint issues candy canes

Where the skies are not cloudy all day
And the deer and the heffalump play
Where little birds fly over the rainbow
And connect with a sweet frog they know

Out there – way way out there
Beyond the Blue

Out there – way way out there - Beyond the Sea
Bobby Darren waits for me

Pack your bags and we'll be on our way
Bring your ukulele and we'll sing and play

Pack your bags and when we get there
I'll buy you bonnie blue ribbons for your bonnie brown hair

Let me take you down cause I'm going to
Somewhere where dreams come true
Somewhere way, way out there

Somewhere . . . way out there

http://www.youtube.com/watch?v=Gx7QEIl459M
Search: # 23 - Out There, Somewhere

Back This Way Again

Well, I don't think I'll be comin' back this way again
I don't think I'll be comin' back this way again
But I'm awful glad I got to see you one more time again my friend
'Cause I don't think I'll be comin' back this way again

I've done my time
I've sung my rhyme
I've did my show
But for everything you start, well Folks
There comes a time to go

And I don't think I'll be comin' back this way again
I don't think I'll be comin' back this way again

    But I'll remember you
    You can try to remember me too
    'Cause I don't think I'll be comin' back this way again
    I don't think I'll be comin' back this way again

I've done my time
I've sung my rhyme
I've did my show
But for everything you start
There comes a time to go

And I don't think I'll be comin' back this way again
I don't think I'll be comin' back this way again

    But I'll remember you
    And won't you try to remember me too
    'Cause I don't think I'll be comin' back this way again
    I don't think I'll be comin' back this way again

    I'll remember you
    Won't you try real hard to remember me too
    'Cause I don't think I'll be comin' back this way again

And I'm awful glad I got to see you one more time again my friend

http://www.youtube.com/watch?v=ztVqFy3DcxQ
Search: # 100b The End - "Back This Way Again"

NOTES

P. 2 -   I've Never Been to Stuckey's
As a lad my Aunt Sis took my brother and me to Florida, driving non-stop from Ohio (except for potty breaks). It seemed like every ten feet was a billboard advertising Stuckey's and its giant (in the picture on the billboard) "*Pecan Log.*" We NEVER stopped. A few years ago, I found a lonely Stuckey's in Indiana and had a *Pecan Log* !! It would have tasted much better and seemed much bigger when I was ten.

P. 3 -   Bird Man
There is a real Bird Man. He lives in London. Look for the film "Ground Floor Right" by Marlene Schlott Rasmussen.

P. 8 -   Lazy Boy
A brand-name reclining chair

P. 11 -   Reading Twain and Bukowski
I read *Huckleberry Finn* one summer during elementary school and loved Twain ever since. A few years back a friend in the UK introduced me to Bukowski. And that was that.

P. 12 -   Latest Word from Head Quarters
This popped into my head once while I was driving. It stayed there long enough to get home and write it down.

P. 13 -   I Wish I Were a Pirate
I call this my Carl Jung song. Isn't it obvious why?

P. 14 -   When I Die
Too many ministers see a funeral as an opportunity to recruit: "If you ever want to see Joe again, you'd better start getting to church." I tell people just the opposite if they want to see me again. I'm going to hell with Huckleberry Finn.

P. 15 -   A Tub of Buttons
Everybody should have one!

P. 16 -   Provincetown
A wonderful place on old Cape Cod.

P. 17 -   Pogo Shtick
Pogo is a cartoon Possum. He said, "We have met the enemy and he is us." The piece was written during the administration of George W. Bush.

P. 19 - Smoking Marijuana Can Cause Mental Illness
Inspired by a newspaper story with the headline: "Smoking Marijuana Can Cause Mental Illness"

P. 25 - Let's Build a Mountain
An OSU architecture grad student tried to get this project going in Flatland Columbus, but the Chamber frowned upon it. They preferred a mountain of garbage and trash.

P. 26 - Union Maid
A song built on Woody Guthrie's song but adjusted for teachers. Our local union was headed toward a possible strike. We sang this song on the steps of the County Courthouse and got a decent settlement.

P. 29 - Stagecoach BBQ
A 30 second radio ad for a great BBQ joint that has since burned down.

P. 36 - Everyday Low Prices at Wal Mart
"Consumption" used to be a disease.

P. 38 - Barnyard in the Sky
See George Orwell's *Animal Farm*

Pp. 41- 46 Headin' for the Moon
         Yo Soy Abuelo
         My Name Is Frances   } - These six are all inspired by my
         I'm Gwendolyn Josephine   grandchildren.
         Rich
         Oh, A.J.

P. 56 - Our Glorious Virtual Reality [everything depends]
Take the Red Pill

P. 56 - Polar Bears
Columbus North High School grads will see a connection.

P. 57 - Graduation Day
I taught 31 years - 21 in a small town district.

P. 60 - Pee Wee Where Have You Gone
Pee Wee was framed (I have thoroughly investigated the matter).

P. 67 - Oscar Mayer DeWine - Mike DeWine, The Wiener the World Awaited

P. 68 - The Day That Superman Died
He did die: *Superman (vol. 2)* #75 in 1992

P. 69 - Stuporman
Written during the administration of George W. Bush

P. 70 - A Package for James in England
Columbus, Ohio is headquarters for White Castle Hamburgers - http://www.whitecastle.com

P. 73 - Thank God for Toilets -
An eighth grade boy (who claimed he was related to Willard Scott) one day suggested (I don't know why), "Mr. Harker, you ought to write a song called, 'Thank God for Toilets.' " Eventually I did.

P. 74 - Booger
Circleville is in Pickaway County; I live one block from Pickaway Street. Burger ("Booger") Hospital really does sit at 600 Pickaway Street: http://www.bergerhealth.com/find-us/

P. 75 - Bonnie Beaver
Don't ask.

P. 77 - Niagara Viagra
After losing the election, at some point Bob Dole became a spokesman for Viagra.

P. 78 - Holy Roller Polka
David Duke is a White-Supremacist who, among other things, ran for governor of Louisiana.

P. 83 - Crazy Over You
This song developed from some chords I learned from a NYC friend, Jason Tagg.

P. 84 - Spam Eatin' Blues
Inspired by a mobile spam-sandwich stand at the Mall of America

P. 85 - Monster In the White House
George W. Bush (actually, Dick Cheney, "Bush's Brain")

P. 86 - Dick Army
Dick Armey of Texas once called Barney Frank "Barney Fag."

P. 89 - I Like Your Haircut
Inspired by an underhanded gink on the school board with a bad attitude and a peanut-shaped head.

P. 91 - Eldorado
Dedicated to my deceased 1984 Eldorado. May she rest in pieces.

P. 94 - Sittin' Down at Shifty's
A real place, good people!

P. 96 - Redwood Tree
I visited Muir Woods and a giant redwood had recently fallen across the visitors' path and had had a big chunk taken out of its trunk to allow us to enter. Farther up the gentle slope the trees still stood - like pillars in a Gothic Cathedral. Then the Muse took over and wrote the song.

P. 98 - I Had a Dream Last Night
A reaction to a Woodstock song.

P. 99 - Left Behind
"Hey-Diddly-Ho, Neighbor!"

P. 102 - Sacramental Wine
From the St. Christopher's elementary school days. Based on two true stories from my best friend (and altar boy) Bill McNamara.

P. 102 - Diffusion
I miss her.

P. 104 - I'll Fly Away
A song for my Old Dad.

PP. 108-9 - John Kasich / Tower in the Sky / Gov. Johnny Kasich's Nightmare Cafe
This guy scores high on the Psychopath Test. He told Ohioans to get on his bus or he'd run us over.

P. 113 - Goodbye Larry's (26a Finished Version)
What a loss! An icon replaced by a plastic restaurant. Don Bovy sang "Batman" there with my band.

P. 117 - Dr. Jekyll Had Something to Hide
A "thank you" to Dan Dougan, who "doesn't golf and he ain't no Mason."

P. 118 - Skinhead Ariisin'
Way back at the beginning of what eventually became part of the Tea Party.

P. 120 - Got Myself a Parrot
The *Columbus Dispatch*, "Ohio's Greatest Ho Newspaper"

P. 131 - Pea Green Boat
See Edward Lear's "The Owl and the Pussycat"

P. 137 - Back This Way Again - Love to all . . .

About the Guilty Parties

Poetry, Lyrics, and Prose: P. Thomas Harker

Phenton Thomas "Ukulele Man" Harker bought a used, pawn shop ukulele at the age of fourteen. You can decide, at this late date, whether or not he has learned how to play it.

Along the way he taught junior and senior high school for thirty-one years, served as the local teachers' union president for fifteen years, led a band - "Ukulele Man & his Prodigal Sons" - for ten years, wrote a lot of songs and poems and rants, made two CD's (available digitally from CD Baby) - *SumoNinjaLele* and *Crazy Old World* - and compiled an ebook, "Ukulele Man's Song Book," containing thirty of his songs (available via Amazon and other distributers).

He lives in Circleville, Ohio - not far from Booger Hospital

Art by M.H. Israel

Martin Harvey Israel has at various times taught math, taught programming, sold insurance, sold stocks, sold antiques, and leapt tall buildings in a single bound.

His Fortress of Solitude is in Flushing, New York.